DESERT SOUTHWEST

GARDENS

AMERICAN DESIGN

DESERT SOUTHWEST

GARDENS

TEXT BY PAULA PANICH AND NORA BURBA TRULSSON
PHOTOGRAPHS BY TERRENCE MOORE
INTRODUCTION BY DR. ROBERT G. BREUNING,
EXECUTIVE DIRECTOR, DESERT BOTANICAL GARDEN
DESIGN BY B. W. HONEYCUTT
Produced by The Miller Press

BANTAM BOOKS • NEW YORK • TORONTO • LONDON • SYDNEY • AUCKLAND

DESERT SOUTHWEST GARDENS
A Bantam Book
October 1990

Library of Congress Cataloging-in-Publication Data

Panich, Paula.
Desert southwest gardens / text by Paula Panich and Nora
Burba Trusson; photos by Terrence Moore; introduction
by Dr. Robert G. Breunig; produced by The Miller
Press, Inc.
    p.   cm.—(American design)
Includes bibliographical references.
    ISBN 0-553-05735-9
1. Architecture, Domestic—Southwest, New.   2.
Gardens—Southwest, New.   I. Trulsson, Nora
Burba.   II. Title.   III. Series.
        NA7224.6.P36   1990
728'.37'097909154—dc20   90-31124
                                            CIP

Published simultaneously in the United States and Canada

---

*Bantam Books are published by Bantam Books, a division of
Bantam Doubleday Dell Publishing Group, Inc. Its
trademark, consisting of the words "Bantam Books" and the
portrayal of a rooster, is Registered in U.S. Patent and
Trademark Office and in other countries. Marca Registrada.
Bantam Books, 666 Fifth Avenue, New York, New York
10103.*

Printed in Italy by New Interlitho S.p.A.-Milan

0 9 8 7 6 5 4 3 2 1

ACKNOWLEDGMENTS

During the course of putting together this book, we strived to showcase a variety of gardens and outdoor living spaces that reflect the diversity of the Southwestern desert regions. In finding these landscapes—both traditional and contemporary—we received the help of dozens of people, many of whom went beyond the call of duty to bring us the gardens found on the following pages.

First, we would like to thank the homeowners, landscape architects, designers, gardeners, architects, and builders whose houses and landscapes are featured in this book. With good humor and many pots of coffee, they let us into their gardens at the crack of dawn and often sat with us at twilight as we raced to capture the perfect moment of golden light across a flowerbed or portal. They endured countless questions and phone calls, and often helped research a fact or two. Without them, there would not have been a book.

We are deeply indebted to our project editor, Sharon Squibb, who kept us on track and on time; to Angela Miller, who believed we could do it again; and to the staff of The Miller Press. Our thanks go to Coleen O'Shea, Beth Kugler, and Becky Cabaza of Bantam Books; and to B.W. Honeycutt and the fine design and production team who made dreams and talk into reality.

Those who helped us along the way include Melanie Peters and Donald Random Murphy, Ann Shelton, Patricia Moorten, Bill and Ann Bolinger, Ken Ronchetti, Linda Campbell, Rick Klein, Abigail Adler, Michael Bliss, Heather Fleck, Tina Stilb, and Tania Messina of The Coyote's Voice in Tucson. We are appreciative of their suggestions, introductions and the time they spent with us.

Thanks also to Bill Field, Anna Kelly, Walt Rogers, Duncan McCandless, Frank Mascia, James Abell, Jane Dolan, Juanita Panich, Judith Phillips, Josie Young, and Jeffrey Stone. We are especially appreciative of the insights given to us by Baker Morrow; by K. Paul Zygas and Madis Pihlak of Arizona State University's College of Architecture and Environmental Design; and by Gretchen M. Pelletier of *San Diego Home/Garden* Magazine.

Additionally, we would like to acknowledge the support of Joel and Lila Harnett, Manya Winsted, Barbara Glynn Denney, Deborah Paddison, and the staff of *Phoenix Home & Garden* Magazine; the expertise of Craig Pearson and Pam Singleton; and the understanding owners and staff of the Keating House Inn in San Diego.

Finally, we would like to dedicate this book to Suzi Moore, Jorgen Trulsson, and "Za moj drug, WDL," for their faith and love.

Paula Panich
Nora Burba Trulsson
Terry Moore

New Mexico

Contents

DESERT SOUTHWEST

GARDENS

INTRODUCTION

The American Southwest is a land of enormous contrasts, ranging in elevation from below sea level to over thirteen thousand feet. The region is characterized by mountains, canyons, mesas, and plateaus, all interspersed with river valleys. There are also characteristics that unify the region. Among these are a sense of vast openness, intense sunlight, and aridity. These are the features that set the Southwest apart. Living in this land requires a generous use of shade. Here rain and snow are the treasured gifts of nature—no experienced Southwesterner takes them lightly. The vast open vistas give the coming of that rain an unparalleled drama. Ask people what they most vividly remember about the Southwest and they will tell you, "the clouds, those incredible clouds."

Human beings have lived on this land for at least fifteen thousand years and over the millennia have developed cultural systems finely turned to the rhythms of nature. The ancient peoples of the Southwest knew the land intimately, and they identified themselves with the land. For example, one of the Indian peoples of southern Arizona called themselves the Desert People—Tohono O'odham. For them the natural setting of the desert was not some barren, depauperate wasteland that had to be survived; it was a rich home. They knew almost four hundred species of plants for use as food alone. This understanding of the land has been all too absent in recent times. European-derived cultures of the modern era have tended to view the Southwestern desert lands as inhospitable places—places to be manipulated and transformed into something more familiar to the European eye. Southwestern city landscapes have become dominated by the rectangular patch of grass and the tall broadleaf tree, no matter how out of place and inappropriate these forms may be in open and arid places.

What Paula Panich, Nora Burba Trulsson, and Terrence Moore have assembled in *Desert Southwest Gardens* is a remarkable group of homes and landscapes that define the essence of an integrated Southwestern landscape and architectural style. These gardens are found in diverse settings ranging from the mountains near Taos, New Mexico, to the Rio Grande River Valley near Albuquerque; to the desert foothills near Phoenix and Tucson; and to Palm Springs and San Diego, California. Each garden consists of well-balanced combinations of native and nonnative plant materials that fit harmoniously into their surroundings and honor the character of the land. These gardens demonstrate a lack of rigid formality, self-consciousness, and pretension. They are all places where you would want to *live*. They were created with carefully designed transitions from the surrounding natural landscapes into the more intimate and shadier spaces next to the homes. The element that strikes you about the gardens in this book is that the owners have found ways to extend their daily lives into the out-of-doors, living comfortably and compatibly with the land around them. These homes and landscapes point the way to a lifestyle to which we all ought aspire—a way in which architecture is carefully integrated into the land and where well-designed gardens provide year-round color, shade, a sense of naturalness, and balance. These are elements that anyone can create on almost any site with the proper amount of sensitivity and imagination. *Desert Southwest Gardens* is a positive inspiration towards that end. When I finished this book, my mind filled with fresh ideas; I wanted to grab my shovel, plant a shade tree or a colorful shrub, and get gardening again.

Dr. Robert G. Breunig
Executive Director
Desert Botanical Garden

E X I C O

New Mexico is an old and fabled land. Tales of its past have captured the imaginations of generations, and the very shape of the land draws more and more people to explore its boundaries.

The mountains of New Mexico are constantly at play with color and light, and there are but few places in the state where they cannot be seen. The Rocky Mountains enter New Mexico around Taos in the north. They rise above 13,000 feet and are covered with snow for much of the year. Rich forests are spread beneath the high peaks, and the land is drained by ancient glacial gorges glittering with waterfalls and lakes. Above 12,000 feet tiny alpine flowers bloom in lush color in spring.

The often gentle, yet sometimes roaring, Rio Grande snakes and slices its way through many of the mountains of New Mexico. The river enters the state in the north through one of the most beautiful gorges on earth. The river is the cradle of New Mexico's civilization, and its rich alluvial plain runs the 470-mile length of the state.

In the south, mountains of lower altitudes rise in the desert—and frame some of the most spectacular skies in New Mexico. Here sunsets can be a burst of heliotrope and peach, ringed with charcoal, just before a quick-falling darkness.

It is no wonder the native people of New Mexico found the mountains to be sacred. Tschicoma (Santa Clara Peak) is the highest peak in the Jemez Range, northwest of Santa Fe on the west side of the Espanola Valley. The mountain, called "the place of much rock" by the Tewa-speaking Indians, was once crowned with an important shrine. This holy place was considered to be the heart of the Pueblo world.

The Pueblo Indians today occupy several pueblo towns in the Rio Grande Valley. The northern-most is Taos Pueblo, which has been occupied by the

Tewa-speaking Taos Indians since about 1400.

The early Pueblo Indians cultivated maize and other crops and used the region's abundant native plants for food and medicine. While Europe was coming toward the end of the Middle Ages, Pueblo Indians at Chaco Canyon's Pueblo Bonito developed a ditch irrigation system.

The first Spanish explorers came to the area from Spanish Mexico in 1534. By the end of the century the subjugated native people were cultivating exotic vineyards, orchards, and vegetables for mission friars.

The Spanish had developed a way of life centering around plazas and terraces in their homeland, and were likely shocked to find the formal landscape tradition in Mexico's Aztec capital when they arrived in the early 1500s. The first Montezuma built a remarkable botanical garden, Chapultepec, which was thriving by the mid-fifteenth century. As has happened in many cultural traditions throughout the Americas, where the culture of the conquerors merges with that of the native people, in Mexico Aztec and Spanish traditions came together to produce formal plazas, patios, and church forecourts.

These ideas came with the conquistadors and padres into New Mexico—to a degree. New Mexico is not the subtropical and tropical paradise of Mexico. Plantings, by necessity, had to be altered for its mostly desert climate.

The modern landscapes of New Mexico bear the mark of decisions made over four centuries ago by the Spanish monarchy. According to landscape architect and historian Baker Morrow, "[King] Philip decreed that all the plazas of his realm were to be laid out in a 2:3 ratio of width to length, and that portales (long, protected arcades or colonades) were to be constructed along building fronts facing any plaza to better serve commerce." The Spanish plazas of New Mexico, built in accordance to Philip's decree, marked the beginnings of civic open spaces based on European models in this part of the New World. Many can still be visited today—the plazas of Santa Fe, Albuquerque, and Taos in the north, and Socorro and Mesilla to the south.

Although the Spanish did not bring ditch irrigation to New Mexico, they did bring the *acequia* system, a water delivery method that was also a microcosm of a traditional social order. Acequias, described at length in a following chapter, still function today in some northern New Mexico communities.

Toward the end of the seventeenth century, the number of Spanish people had grown to 2,000 in "New" Mexico. To support themselves the Spanish demanded tribute—corn, wheat, squash, beans, chilies, tobacco, and cotton—and slave labor from the Pueblo Indians. In 1680 the Pueblo Indians attempted to throw off the invaders in what is known as the Pueblo Revolt.

Twelve years later the Spanish were again in firm control of the Pueblos of New Mexico. The Indians and their conquerors began a period of uneasy coexistence, though Spanish rule was to end when Mexico gained independence from Spain in 1821. Foreigners, especially Anglos, began coming into New Mexico when it became ruled by newly-independent Mexico.

Opened to outside influences for the first time, change was afoot in New Mexico. In 1846 it became a territory of the United States. Its capital city, Sante Fe, and its largest city, Albuquerque, along with smaller towns throughout the territory, were subject to the same architectural influences as Tucson or Phoenix in Arizona—the fashions of mid-nineteenth-century America.

Picket fences, wide grass lawns, and shade trees surrounded Territorial houses (a wonderful mix of mud houses with Greek Revival flourishes) from one end of the territory to the other. Toward the end of the nineteenth century, Victorian houses graced Santa Fe and Albuquerque just as they did San Francisco, Phoenix, or St. Louis, all thanks to the swift delivery by railroad of manufactured building materials.

It was about this time civic leaders in Santa Fe were concerned the city would suffocate under the weight of Victorian bric-a-brac. Pueblo Revival architecture was born to give Santa Fe a new, but "old" look—a nostalgic mix of the traditional building style of the Pueblo Indians and the influence of Spanish taste and style brought to the New World by the conquistadors and friars.

The astute urban planning worked. Santa Fe today is known for its remarkable Pueblo Revival architecture and its thriving economy based on tourism. The Pueblo Revival style was at its full flowering in the 1930s with the influence of John Gaw Meem, whose work at Los Poblanos Ranch in Albuquerque follows in this section. The eclectic landscapes of Los

Poblanos were carefully thought out and executed, modeled on the formalism of the English garden, the vineyards and orchards of the Spanish, and the agricultural traditions of the Rio Grande Valley.

Elsewhere in the state, other influences are found. At the NAN Ranch in the Mimbres Valley in southeastern Grant County, architect Henry Trost built an Italianate villa surrounded by picturesque pools, sculptures, and formal gardens.

The modern era in landscape architecture in the United States is usually attributed to a group of students at the Harvard Graduate School of Design in the 1930s. Garrett Eckbo, Dan Kiley, and others—who were to become the giants of their field in the ensuing decade—were proponents of site-specific design and easy maintenance. The innovations of the Harvard gang were not lost on landscape architects in New Mexico, where an eclectic but recognizable regional style began to blossom.

Bud Hollied, the designer of the 1930s Roosevelt Park in Albuquerque and of Glorieta Gardens near Santa Fe, and Cecil Pragnell, one of the architects of the Los Poblanos landscapes and co-designer of Glorieta Gardens, were among the leaders in developing the Rio Grande style. The regional look is a mix of the enclosed courtyards and fountains of the Spanish, the naturalism of the English, and the irrigation systems, flagstone masonry, small gardens, and adobe wall construction of the Pueblo Indians.

In the 1960s and early seventies, landscape designer Jose Yguado created some of the state's most important urban spaces, and made a significant contribution to the Rio Grande style. He landscaped portions of downtown Central Avenue in Albuquerque and conceived the renovations of the historic plazas of Old Mesilla, Taos, and Socorro.

Recent population growth along the Rio Grande has created water problems for the cities, although dams along the Rio Grande—the Caballo, Elephant Butte, and Cochiti—have so far been able to provide adequate water for both irrigation and urban uses. In preparation for the future growth of Albuquerque and Santa Fe, water has been diverted from the San Juan River into the Chama River, a tributary of the Rio Grande in the north.

Today Albuquerque is a city of just under 500,000, where the summertime highs average about ninety degrees, and in winter the mercury stays a reasonable forty-eight during sunny days. People in Albuquerque love the city's style—in winter it is possible to play golf in the morning and, after a thirty minute drive, to ski in the Sandia Mountains for the afternoon. There are good museums, theater groups, a place to observe the birds and migratory fowl of the Rio Grande, and all manner of other outdoor sports, from river rafting to mountain and valley-bottom hiking to horse racing.

Santa Fe, in the foothills of the Sangre de Cristo Range, is perched on a mesa 7,000 feet above sea level. Surrounded by piñon and juniper forests, the city of 60,000 was named Most Livable Small City in 1987. Its distinctive Pueblo Revival architecture, thriving arts colony, and multi-layered mix of Pueblo Indian, Spanish, and Anglo cultures make it one of the most culturally rich communities in the United States.

The Rio Grande style of landscape design continues to develop in both cities with an increasing use of native plants, thanks to growers and designers like Judith Phillips in Albuquerque. Not only are homeowners and designers concerned with water conservation, many have also become aware of the beauty of native drought-tolerant plants—desert willows, big sage, chamisa (rubber rabbitbrush), and fourwing saltbrush.

Landscape architect Baker Morrow in recent years has been refining his own regional design, the foothills garden in both domestic and commercial landscapes. Using stonework, trickles of water, local plants such as oaks and Mexican elders, among other plantings, and a reinterpretation of nearby hilly topography, Morrow's work is a balance of the formal and informal. Inherent in the ever-developing regional style is the idea that every design must be site-specific, taking its cues from the local geography and concentrating areas of green space with intensive landscaping and making the outlying areas wilder—a xeriscape of unique native plantings.

It is possible in any of New Mexico's climates to create a pleasing landscape without trying to reconstruct the broad lawns of the Midwest in the wide deserts of New Mexico. As grower Judith Phillips observes, compromise is best: "Create a pocket of humus for a few exotics and go native for the balance."

11

Rambling Ranchland

Albuquerque's Historic, Rural Landscape

F ROM THE AIR, Albuquerque's North Valley looks like a sprawling green oasis in the midst of a dusty desert. It has long been nurtured by the ancient Rio Grande, the city's ever-flowing source of life. Albuquerque spreads north and south along the basin of this fabled river, and the city is framed by the Sandia Mountains on its eastern border and by a chain of five extinct volcanoes to the west. Albuquerque was founded in 1706 as a Spanish town for thirty-five families, but record of its human habitation has been traced back 25,000 years.

The Rio Grande closely borders Albuquerque's North Valley, and here it is still possible to see the texture of the city's rural past, stretches of uninterrupted farmland and bosque, a riverside forest of cottonwood trees. Old adobes and lush acreage are snuggled up against suburban housing developments, but much of this valley retains its genus loci, a special spirit of place.

Los Poblanos Ranch has been an important part of the economic, political, and social life of the North Valley for generations. The ranch is believed to be built atop a buried Indian village occupied between A.D. 1300 and 1400. The area was adjacent to a major trail system from the upper Colorado River to the

A welcoming allée of cottonwoods and elms, enlivened by masses of white spiraea blooms in spring in Albuquerque's North Valley (LEFT).

Grazing in winter wheat, a velvety-faced ewe pauses in the front fields of Los Poblanos. Sheep are part of a long tradition on the ranch (ABOVE).

middle Rio Grande Valley that was in use for six centuries by the indigenous people of the region and by the Spanish as well. The area of the ranch shows up in the 1790 Spanish census as San Antonio. By the mid-nineteenth century, Los Poblanos was the home of Vincente Armijo, whose family was to become wealthy and politically influential in the territory.

The presence of influential inhabitants in Los Poblanos Ranch continued with its purchase in 1929 by Albert Simms, a congressman from New Mexico, and Ruth Hanna McCormick Simms, former congresswoman from Illinois. She was the daughter of Senator Mark Hanna of Ohio and the widow of another U.S. senator.

Ruth Simms made the acquaintance of one of the Southwest's most important architects, John Gaw Meem, several years before she moved to New Mexico. He remodeled Los Poblanos' existing 1850s farmhouse into a gracious Territorial Revival-style hacienda. The house is built around a central *placita,* or outdoor square, and has straight walls, sharp corners, and dentilated brick coping on the roofline—all common to the celebrated style.

The house is approached by a long, lush drive, shaded by a

canopy of towering cottonwoods and elms. The house's main entry is on the east, where the architect designed a graceful wall punctuated by large, double-hung wood sash windows, framed in glossy white wood and crowned with pediments. A portal paved with pink San Cristobal flagstone runs the full length of the facade.

According to New Mexican architecture historian Bainbridge Bunting, Meem used the existing house for bedrooms and servants' quarters, and built a new wing on the east for the living room, entrance, and master suite. The Simms' remodeled twelve room house was based on the idea of an old-fashioned New Mexican hacienda with interconnecting rooms around the open patio. Under the portal surrounding the placita, the new owners built an outdoor living room with a fireplace.

The architect also designed the garage complex and separate servants' quarters, a delightful Territorial-style building the current owners use as a guest house. The formal gardens of Los Poblanos, laid out in the 1930s and continued sixty years later, is another example of the cross-culturalization often seen in New Mexico. Located behind and to the west of the U-shaped house,

15

Creamy Lady Banksia roses festoon the interior portals around the outdoor central placita (LEFT). A luncheon table is set with cobalt blue dishes and a vivid tablecloth hand-embroidered with whimsical animals. The placita is the heart of the hacienda; the family passes through this outdoor living space to enter the major rooms of the house.

Along an adobe wall, a wrought-iron garden chair from Mexico offers rest (TOP LEFT). The delicate design on the back of the chair depicts the seasons of spring and summer.

A reflecting pond on the south side of the raised beds of the garden is filled with water from the Rio Grande (TOP RIGHT).

the gardens are a fanciful mix of a formal English garden and New Mexican folk art. The garden was designed in 1933 by landscape architect Rose Greeley and further developed by New Mexican landscape pioneer Cecil Pragnell. Its formality is in counterpoint to the pebble designs on the pathways and fountain made by New Mexican folk artist "Pop" Shaeffer.

Just as the work on the house was being completed, Ruth Simms employed the architect to plan another structure on the property, to be called La Quinta. The building was to be the Simms' entertainment center—a U-shaped structure built around a swimming pool, with a seventy-foot ballroom, an art gallery, and an enormous library. It was a semipublic building as the Simms were patrons of the arts. They entertained lavishly here, and for many years La Quinta was the site of Albuquerque's June Music Festival.

Albert Simms established a successful dairy on the ranch and developed pure-bred Holstein cattle. Los Poblanos, then 435 acres, quickly became the major force in the economic life of the North Valley.

The ranch stayed in the Simms' family until it was sold to Armin and Penny Rembe. The couple moved to Los Poblanos in 1978 with their four young children. The property still retained its 1930s appearance with a few exceptions. In the 1960s, an open, flagstone-paved portal behind the kitchen was enclosed with large windows, and a lagoon was added to the east of the main house.

The new owners quickly discovered the placita to be the heart of the house, both visually and spiritually. It is an outdoor living space through which the family must pass to enter any of the major rooms in the house. Its centerpiece is a tiled fountain in the shape of a six-pointed star, fed by pure, fresh well water. The hand-painted, mostly blue and yellow tiles of the fountain show bullfighting scenes and country life. The Rembes believe the tiles are from Spain.

The placita and the extra-wide north portal are paved with a basketweave brick pattern set with small carved tiles. Underneath the north portal is a traditional adobe fireplace. The Rembes have arranged this area with a table and chairs used for outdoor din-

ing, and it is open to winter sun, evidence of the architect's early awareness of the importance of sun angles in the siting of houses of New Mexico.

In 1986, the Rembes planted creamy, pale yellow Lady Banksia (the yellow variety is also known as Lutea) roses on all four sides of the placita's portal. In the spring, thousands of the tiny roses, which grow in clusters like small bouquets, festoon the top of the portal, adding a blossom canopy to the existing small trees and shrubs of the interior courtyard. Birds dip in to visit (a strategically placed plastic snake in the roses have discouraged them lately) and ducks shoot straight ahead above the courtyard.

The Rembes bought not only the John Gaw Meem-designed structures but also a greenhouse with a glazed gambrel roof that opens to a potting shed, two small gabled buildings used for wine-pressing and as the entrance to an underground wine cellar, and a complex of dairy buildings: a dairy sales room, an enormous open-sided gambrel-roofed barn of corrugated metal, and two silos that were used for storage of feed grain. There are also

old gasoline pumps, a foreman's cottage, and sheds for the sheep and dogs.

Under the stewardship of the Rembes, Los Poblanos has continued to thrive as an architectural and horticultural masterpiece. The ranch is not a museum, but a rich and varied property where the lushness of the North Valley continues to be enjoyed by the Rembe family and their friends and acquaintances.

The elaborate west garden, originally laid out in the 1930s, is abloom each spring as it has been for more than a half-century with the jewel-like colors of peonies, hundreds of rose bushes, and irises; the Rembes have added dahlias, sweet rocket, delphiniums, Queen Anne's lace, and larkspur. At the east end of the garden a small bridge rises above a semicircular pond. From this body of water a narrow channel runs down the center of a path leading to a square fountain. The water comes forth from a cupid holding a shell above his head. It is surrounded by wide-mouthed frogs the Rembes have placed along the edge of the fountain. At the south end of the garden folk artist "Pop"

On the west side of the placita, in beds planted with shrubs and flowers, are the garden statuary images of Maximillian and Carlotta, the European emperor and empress of Mexico from 1864 to 1867. The Mexican antique statues were a gift to the owners (FAR TOP LEFT and RIGHT).

A patient concrete lion listens to a perpetual chorus of frogs from Mexico (FAR TOP MIDDLE). Water from the Rio Grande travels from the pond into channels to the fountain on the placita.

Pebbles set in concrete form delightful paths through the formal garden, the stonework of the late folk artist "Pop" Shaeffer (LEFT).

19

Shaeffer's whimsical work—pebble animals—are set in concrete all along the edge. (Greeley's original blueprint plans for this garden are mounted in the workroom of the greenhouse.)

A rose arbor serves as an entry to another landscape. Adjacent to the west garden is a meadowlike space outside the master bedroom wing, ringed with sycamores, cottonwoods, and elms.

For the first five years the Rembes lived at Los Poblanos, landscape gardener Robert Squires assisted the family's longtime gardener, Jesus Holguin, in the planting and restoration of the gardens. In the 1930s as many as twelve gardeners worked at Los Poblanos. During the winter, Holguin manages the gardens and landscape himself, and in the summer he is assisted by another full-time gardener along with the Rembes.

The landscapes at Los Poblanos were designed to harmonize with the agricultural aspects of the ranch. Between the house and the farm buildings are lawns, tall cottonwoods, the cutting garden (planted with peonies and about every other flower grown in

the west garden), a grape arbor, vegetable gardens, masses of blackberries, and a fruit tree orchard (pears, peaches, and cherries planted eight years ago) bordered by an espalier.

The greenhouse is chockablock with hundreds of enormous geraniums and houses most of Los Poblanos' potted perennials in winter. The structure is edged along its south side with an herb garden, as Penny Rembe once grew herbs commercially for one of her many business interests. The other existing agricultural buildings are used variously for storage and to serve the animals still kept on the ranch.

Penny Rembe is a passionate vegetable gardener, and has a feeling for the land of the North Valley that was nurtured by her girlhood experiences on her family's ranch. She does the planning and seeding of the vegetable garden in April. She plants ornamental cabbage and kale for borders, and specialty vegetables such as baby corn and baby beets are planted along with lettuces, radishes, and carrots in a "salad bowl" area of the gar-

A path cuts its way through a wide expanse of lawn and ends at the 1930s greenhouse, which is crowned with a glazed gambrel roof (LEFT). The building opens to a stuccoed potting shed, where the current owners display the original plans for the garden as conceived by Rose Greeley in 1933.

A Chinese lotus (*Nelumbo nucifera*) is abloom in the lagoon. The small body of water has been used in the past by the Rio Grande Zoo as part of a breeding program for endangered species of wildfowl (TOP RIGHT).

Queen Anne's lace and other spring blossoms grace the formal English garden laid out in the 1930s (FAR TOP RIGHT). It is believed the garden once included the only parterre in New Mexico.

The formal garden (here, with cosmos in bloom) is bordered on the north by a storage/garage complex, also designed by John Gaw Meem in 1932 (BOTTOM RIGHT). The building has a high-ceilinged room with a room-sized twelve-foot-high wooden cooler, once used for vegetables and fruits.

Elegant geese dip into the ranch's lagoon for a swim among the lotus plants (FAR BOTTOM RIGHT).

den. She mixes herbs and flowers in with the vegetables for natural insect resistance, and masses plants together in wide beds to conserve water and cut down on weeds. Penny also plants Japanese eggplant, small pumpkins, Mexican corn, and a "salsa" collection of tomatoes, chiles, cilantro, and peppers.

In the spring, trunks of the enormous cottonwoods and elms along the entry drive to Los Poblanos' main house are alight with thousands of white spiraea blossoms. Meadowlarks dive in and out of the shiny new cottonwood leaves singing their sweet songs. To the north of the drive, sheep—seventeen ewes, two rams, and eighteen lambs—graze in a field of winter wheat. The sheep are part of a long tradition at Los Poblanos; throughout the years members of the Navajo tribe would come to the ranch to buy lambs. From time to time, a few Pueblo Indians still do.

It is likely a visitor to the ranch will hear the startling, deep-throated cry of peacocks and then will see an exquisite male (one of ten of the birds living at Los Poblanos), whose morning ritual is to stand on the roof of the main house. He is in full view of the placita, making sure he is seen by all who happen to pass by.

Geese and mallards (200 of them zip through the bosque in winter) along with other wild ducks are either in residence at the ranch or pass over it; the fenced lagoon has been used by the Rio Grande Zoo as part of their breeding program for endangered wildfowl species.

In 1986 the Rembes planted lotus plants in the lagoon. In mid-August, the small body of water is abloom with the exotic white flowers, lending a Japanese-like tranquility to the surrounding landscape.

In many ways the Rembes have continued the social and political heritage of Los Poblanos. The couple often entertains large groups of people, raising funds for political candidates, hosting botanical garden and house tours, and opening the house and garden to a constant stream of schoolchildren learning about the history of Albuquerque.

Irrigation for the gardens, lawns, and fields of Los Poblanos takes place on Mondays. The ranch is fed through a system of *acequias* (irrigation ditches) from the nearby Rio Grande, as it has been for centuries. The fields and lawns are mowed on Fridays, and often much of Saturday too. The Rembes try to schedule school tours in warm weather on irrigation day. Then children can remove their shoes and run through the river water on the lawns at Los Poblanos as generations have done before them.

Historic Waterway

A Flowing Acequia in the Upper Santa Fe River Canyon

EFORE AUTOMOBILES, the Upper Santa Fe River Canyon was a farming community, separate from Santa Fe. Spanish families in the piñon-studded canyon grew chiles, raised goats, operated stills and a community sawmill, and tended apple, peach, and cherry orchards—all made possible by the life-giving water of the Santa Fe River delivered through a system of *acequias*, or irrigation ditches. The Upper Canyon is now a residential neighborhood far above the mercantile busyness of Santa Fe's center.

Booker and Susan Kelly have lived in a traditional Pueblo-style adobe house on the north side of the Upper Santa Fe River Canyon since 1962. It is the quintessential Santa Fe house, having grown from its humble mud beginnings 160 years ago to an elegant, L-shaped family dwelling.

Booker Kelly's family came to Santa Fe in the 1880s, part of the wave of Anglo-Americans arriving with the railroad. Susan Kelly is a native of Santa Fe as well, and both treasure childhood memories of a quieter Santa Fe, a small village filled with the intoxicating aroma of piñon smoke. The historic house was an ideal purchase for the Kellys. The oldest part of the house dates

Wide wooden shutters, original to the Kelly house, are painted in traditional Santa Fe blue (LEFT).

Geraniums add color to the high desert surrounding the house. Flagstone stairs set with tile lead to a parking area that is separated from the landscape of the house by a low adobe wall (ABOVE).

A fir Taos bed, a wedding gift to the owners, is placed strategically next to the portal's rounded fireplace (LEFT).

At the blue-trimmed kitchen door at the front of the house, the owners' cat pauses on the flagstone porch (ABOVE LEFT).

San Isidro, a painting by Susan Harrison Kelly of the patron saint of farmers, plays with the colors of the window and chair beneath the portal, which is the family's summer living room (ABOVE RIGHT).

from the 1830s, but the land on which it was built was granted to the Rodriguez family (whose descendants still live in the Upper Canyon) by the king of Spain in the late eighteenth century.

The property was divided and subdivided by Rodriguez family wills for generations; this particular house was first sold outside the family in the 1940s.

When acquired by the present owners, the rounded adobe house had grown beyond its first two early nineteenth-century rooms. In the 1940s the house was plumbed and electrified and a new entry, pantry, and bedroom were added. The Kellys built further, adding a living room, bedroom, bath, and hallway in 1963 and extending the existing portal, or porch, so that it runs the full length of the living room and bedroom wings in the back of the house.

The Kellys created a detached guest house from an old garage in 1975. It is situated up the hill above the house, nearer to the street. The family—the Kellys raised three children in the main house—refers to the guest house as the "upstairs." The structure

is now used by Susan Kelly as her painting studio, although it can still function as an extra bedroom.

From the street, the house is accessible through a gravel parking area outside the studio and also along flagstone stairs running to the front door of the house. From the studio, there are stairs to the kitchen door. The front of the house is landscaped with clean, simple lines—rocks surrounding trees and shrubs, contained flowerbeds, and pots of blooming flowers. Near the house is a wide, well-established bed of June-blooming dark blue iris along with beds of blue mountain flax, valerian, candytuft, and blue snow-in-summer. Two apple trees—one bearing pale winesaps, the other red delicious—thrive here as well. Pots of bright geraniums and other flowers are strategically placed by the flagstone stairs and near the blue-trimmed kitchen door.

When the Kellys bought the house, the back garden ended at the acequia. A "coyote" fence, common to northern New Mexico and made of slender saplings, was built around 1965, and what later became known as the lower garden, between the acequia and the fence, was cultivated during a three year period in the mid-sixties.

Virginia creeper now covers the coyote fence, having found its way there on its own. Ubiquitous in Santa Fe, the vine helps to support the sapling fence. Its brilliant red color in late autumn is a harbinger of the first frost of winter.

Outside the fence, Chinese elms and Lombardy poplars have grown into mature trees in the last twenty years—other gifts from mother nature.

The lower garden has been planted, with some exceptions, with flowering plants indigenous to the Southwest. Along the fence are yellow and blue columbine, multicolored gaillardias,

Ripening apples shine in the late summer sun at the front of the residence; they will soon be ready for harvesting (FAR LEFT).

The curving ditch of the acequia runs through the back of the property (MIDDLE LEFT). The acequia system was brought to northern New Mexico by the Spanish in the late sixteenth century. Today the acequia on the north part of the Upper Santa Fe Canyon is kept in running order for the sake of tradition.

The pine table set with Italian pottery plates and Mexican cobalt blue glassware is ready for a buffet luncheon (LEFT).

29

pink cosmos, zinnias, chrysanthemums, and yarrow. A small area is devoted to cucumbers and tomatoes each year.

The upper and lower gardens are separated by a flagstone walkway. On the upper level are carnations, daisies, yellow candytuft, orange colingulas, red and purple petunias, nasturtiums, Shasta daisies, and daylilies. The owners plant annuals and the passionately cultivated vegetables on the full moon closest to June first—for only then can gardeners in the Upper Canyon feel certain the danger of frost has passed. In June, the garden is a riot of color, and by late July it has reached its crest of beauty. Beyond the two-level garden is a magnificent view of the piñon and juniper forested ridge and the lush canyon below.

In the spring and summer, the Kellys use their gracious portal as an extended living room. Framed by a giant Russian olive tree, the portal is where they often entertain.

The portal is comfortable and pleasing. A fir Taos bed, a traditional northern New Mexico furniture form, was made by a friend and given to the Kellys in 1960 as a wedding gift. It is as wide as a single bed and is the centerpiece of the portal's seating. A pine dining table is surrounded by assorted hand-painted Mexican chairs. Susan Kelly's artistic eye is evident in the aesthetically pleasing details of the portal. Her collection of found objects shares a weathered redwood table with a collection of potted succulents to the side of the portal's rounded, tiled fireplace.

The outdoor space enjoyed by the owners is made all the more interesting by the rare, still-functioning acequia running through the backyard. The acequia firmly links the house to its nineteenth-century origins. The much needed water the Kellys receive through the ditch nourishes spring and summer grass and the garden.

Acequia refers either to an irrigation ditch or to the association of members—people who actually use the water—organized around the ditch. Each acequia is self-governed by a *comison* (commission) of three landowner *parciantes*, or member-shareholders. The manager, or boss, of an *acequia* is commonly called the *mayordomo*.

On the portal, votive candles sit on the two-tone fireplace beneath a mosaic of tiles from Talavera, Mexico, which form the image of Our Lady of Guadalupe (FAR LEFT).

The clear light of a Santa Fe spring morning shines on the window above the kitchen sink (MIDDLE LEFT). Folk art and cobalt glassware are displayed inside the house and outdoors.

Above the fireplace on the portal, votive candles and a crown of thorns (*Euphorbia milii*), with its clusters of bright red bracts, sit beneath a mosaic of tiles from Talavera, Mexico, which form the image of Our Lady of Guadalupe (ABOVE LEFT).

The soft curves of a buttressed adobe wall are found on the side of the Pueblo-style house (ABOVE).

Booker Kelly is the mayordomo of the Cerro Gordo Acequia in the Upper Canyon. (Each local ditch has its own name, usually a reference to local geography.) In the late twentieth century, water in the Cerro Gordo Acequia is kept flowing in the March through October growing season mostly for tradition's sake. The dozen parciantes in the Cerro Gordo Acequia use the water to irrigate their gardens. If for some reason the water isn't flowing, homeowners along the acequia can turn on their garden hoses, unlike the Upper Canyon farmers only a few decades earlier who depended on acequia-delivered water for their livelihoods.

Once a year, the mayordomo of the Cerro Gordo Acequia organizes the spring cleanup. The ditch is cleared by a crew of parciantes of a winter's growth of willows, roots, and grass, along with the season's accumulation of debris. The parciantes bring shovels and walk the length of the ditch as in days of old.

Blue and ocher tiles from Talavera, Mexico, painted with the image of a woman with a jug, are set in the wall by the kitchen door (LEFT).

Flagstone stairs lead to the front door of the Kelly residence (RIGHT). The front of the house is landscaped with clean, simple lines—rocks surrounding trees and shrubs, contained flowerbeds, and pots of blooming flowers. Near the house is a wide, well-established bed of June-blooming dark blue iris along with beds of blue mountain flax, valerian, candytuft, and blue snow-in-summer.

As a nod to the twentieth century, a backhoe is used to clear the main channel at critical diversion points.

Among the trees and flowers fed by the acequia is a gnarled apple tree that brings forth sour cooking apples Susan Kelly puts to good use in apple muffins. The tree, near the acequia and next to a bush of miniature honeysuckles, dates from the late nineteenth century and still produces well. It is also wise in its old age, always waiting until late May to bloom when there is little chance of frost. The two younger apple trees in the front yard bloom in early May.

Recently, the owners have noticed delicate lines etched in the bark of the old apple tree. The lines are the result of black bears clawing their way up the tree to reach the fruit. There are many fruit trees in the canyon, some left from the orchards of the nineteenth century farmers. The bears still come down from the Sangre de Cristo Range each fall to fatten up for the winter. The yard is visited by a mother bear and her cub, who stop by the apple tree on their way to a lush pear tree in the yard of a neighbor. The bears are a reminder that this was once, after all, a canyon in the wild.

Succulents, rocks, pottery, and pitchfork form a tableau on a weathered redwood table (LEFT). The table was found beneath the old apple tree when the present owners bought the house.

The morning sun greets the lush piñon and juniper forested ridge (TOP RIGHT). The Santa Fe River Canyon rolls on beyond the ridge toward the riverbed. Since 1962, Lombardy poplars, Chinese elms, and box elders have grown up in the canyon. The view across to the mountains is of the foothills of the Sangre de Cristo Range.

An expanse of lawn spreads out in spring and summer from the portal of the house to the acequia and the garden beyond it (RIGHT). The owners extended the existing portal of the 160-year-old home in the 1960s.

Ridgetop Panorama

A Portal with a View in Santa Fe

O<small>N THE BREEZY</small> back portal of the ridgetop Santa Fe house, there are two hammocks, tied between the support posts. From the comfort of the hammocks, one can linger over the pages of a book or, being in a more contemplative frame of mind, watch the summer storm clouds gather over the nearby Sangre de Cristo and Jemez mountain ranges and listen to the wind hiss gently through the branches of the compact junipers on the hillside.

The spacious portal, or porch, is the heart of the house for an outdoors-oriented couple and their guests. From the time the days become warmer in the late spring until the cold is too much to bear in the autumn, the doors are flung open and the outside becomes an extension of the living and dining rooms. The couple, who has eight grown children and, at last count, eighteen grandchildren, had precisely this informal usage in mind when they had the Territorial-style adobe house built in 1980.

Like many native Texans, the homeowners were first attracted to Santa Fe as a vacation spot for its crystalline air, active arts community, and charming adobe architecture. Eventually, they purchased a house near the town's historic

The portal offers front-seat views of the day's last rays (LEFT).

On a ridge dotted with piñon and juniper, the Territorial-style house features a generous north-facing portal. The guest house, on the far left, is a smaller version of the main dwelling (ABOVE).

Inside the entry courtyard, a small bed of petunias adds a splash of color below the living room window. Mown clover is used instead of grass as the courtyard's ground cover. Each summer, the peach tree yields hundreds of small, sweet fruit.

A gravel driveway leads visitors to the front gate, centered between the two wings of the house (LEFT). The crisp lines of the adobe house's detailing signal the Territorial influence. The front flowerbeds, filled with Shasta daisies, cosmos, and the chartreuse-blossomed santolina, serve as a transition between the surrounding natural scrub and the more formally landscaped courtyard and backyard.

center. Though it was more than adequate, it had no real views of the sweeping landscape surrounding the city.

They decided to build, and purchased a hillside lot just north of town in a more rural development, not far from the site of the Santa Fe Opera. The lot, dotted with the juniper and piñon native to this transition zone between the desert and upland regions, has wonderful vistas of the mountains to the northeast and to the west.

Santa Fe architect Victor Johnson was engaged to design a house with a traditional New Mexican theme. He worked with local builder Dennis Saye. Utilizing a simple, Territorial motif, the architect chose adobe as the building material and topped the structure with a pitched, corrugated metal roof common to the houses of northern New Mexico, where snow and rain are climatic factors. Eschewing Pueblo-style architectural hallmarks

such as protruding beams and rounded forms to the walls, the architect's Territorial detailings for the house include mullioned windows, painted white trim, and sharply defined edges to the walls, all signaling a later period in Southwestern architecture.

The house is built into a slight rise in the lot, presenting a low-key appearance to the street. At a lower level of the lot, there is a swimming pool, connected to the portal by a set of stairs. The architect used a U-shaped floor plan, with the wings of the dwelling flanking the entry courtyard. A *zaguan*, or wide entry hall, cuts the house in half and connects the front courtyard with the back portal, which wraps around the house's north and west sides. The zaguan also organizes the house into two distinct zones. On one side, there is a generous country-style kitchen, complete with a fireplace and comfortable seating area, a dining

room, and the master suite. The other half is comprised of the living room and sunny guest bedrooms. The interior features rustic furnishings, many windows and skylights that provide an airy ambience, and hand-applied mud plaster walls.

As appealing as the interior is, the owners' passion for gardening and the demands of an active family led to the creation of an exterior that is equally as livable.

On the street side of the house, just outside of the walled entry courtyard, the flora was left in its natural state of scrub and wild flowers to blend the landscape into the surrounding rural setting. Closer to the house, nature was nudged a bit and wild flowers, ground covers, and other plantings were added for color and erosion control. Fiery-hued gaillardia, Shasta daisies, cosmos, santolina, and flax are welcoming sights for visitors pulling up

on the gravel driveway. Vinca, ajuga, and violets can be spotted around the periphery of the house.

Inside the front courtyard, the owners tend to the more productive aspects of the landscape. With the occasional help of a gardener, they have cultivated a small orchard within protective adobe walls. Freestone peaches, apricots, pears, and Bing cherries find their way into delicious desserts and preserves; beneath the kitchen window, zinnias share space with a cook's garden of savory, fennel, basil, arugula, tomatoes, parsley, thyme, and other seasonal delights. At one end of the courtyard, there was an attempt to cultivate grapes, but the fruit of the vine proved to be too touchy for Santa Fe's 7,000-foot-high altitude. Roses have become a beautiful substitute. In the courtyard, the owners opted for a mown clover ground cover instead of grass.

A weathered wooden gate in the adobe garden wall leads visitors from the front drive into the courtyard (FAR LEFT).

A wide brick pathway leads from the courtyard into the *zaguan*, or entry hall. Inside the zaguan, the table is an eighteenth-century Spanish Colonial piece and the bronze heads are by New York artist Joseph Glasco (MIDDLE LEFT).

Double front doors open to reveal the zaguan, which divides the home into two sections (ABOVE LEFT). Access to the kitchen and access to the living room are on opposite sides of the hallway. Another set of doors opens onto the portal. The transom above the doorway fills the hallway with natural light.

From the zaguan, the northern view across the portal is broad and breathtaking. Summer storms can be seen miles away. The ash rocker is Canadian, with snowshoe leather webbing (ABOVE RIGHT).

The wide portal was designed to accommodate groupings of furniture, creating an outdoor living and dining room. A strip of Plexiglas along the roofline of the portal closet to the house brightens the space. The furniture, mostly American country antiques, is regularly waxed and stays out from the late spring to mid-fall. The decking material is pine planks; the steps lead to a small stretch of lawn (RIGHT).

An old Mexican cross and a vase of wild flowers are the simple adornments along the side wall of the zaguan. The white console is the covering for a radiator. Bits of straw give texture to the mud-plastered walls (BELOW LEFT).

A piñon fire in the portal's fireplace takes the chill off a late afternoon (BELOW MIDDLE). Spent beeswax candles in the spindle candlesticks attest to their frequent use. Using traditional methods, straw was mixed in the mud plaster applied the protected walls of the portal, adding textural interest to the surface. An old cupboard does double duty as a plant stand on the portal (BELOW RIGHT).

The pool, easily accessible from the portal, is set lower on the hillside property (FAR TOP RIGHT). The house's pitched metal roof is typical of northern New Mexico, where snow and rain are climatic factors.

Ever-changing cloud patterns in the summer sky offer compelling reasons to stop swimming and enjoy the view (FAR BOTTOM RIGHT).

If the courtyard is where the owners test their green thumbs, the back portal has become the place where they enjoy the fruits of their labors. Normally the traditional Southwestern portal is narrow—some six to eight feet wide. But the couple wanted theirs to be fully furnished—like an outdoor living and dining area—and requested that the architect make the portal thirteen feet wide. In another twist on tradition, the architect installed a narrow strip of Plexiglas skylight along the edge of the portal's roof closest to the walls of the house. The exterior walls are washed with a gentle light, and the portal is saved from being in perpetual shade. A cozy outdoor fireplace takes the chill off a summer evening. In addition to the zaguan, there is access from the house to the portal through French doors located in the dining room.

On the weathered pine planks of the portal, a collection of American country antiques that the owners have acquired over the years, mostly from antique shops and secondhand stores in Texas, is arranged. Many of the pieces have been refinished by the wife, who sets the furniture out on the portal from the time when the weather warms up, until the first signs of frost.

The guest house has its own small, north-facing portal, brightened with pots of flowers and casual furniture.

A young cottonwood tree glistens in the late afternoon sun along the side of the portal (LEFT). The steps lead down toward the pool.

Just off the kitchen, a long harvest table on the portal is surrounded by a charmingly random collection of chairs. This creates an inviting setting for dinners al fresco. At the other end of the portal, ash rockers, a handful of old student chairs from Texas A & M University, a carved bench, and the two colorful hammocks lure visitors to sit a spell and watch the rabbits scamper across a small stretch of lawn. Simple accessories add just the right finishing touch to the portal: pots of red geraniums, a Mexican wooden bowl, and an area rug woven by one of the couple's daughters.

The layout of the house and its landscape work well for the owners. Entertaining means family-style breakfasts on the weathered harvest table, informal dinners, or cocktail gatherings with neighbors. When the double doors are thrown open at

either end of the zaguan, guests can circulate between the court-yard and portal, the kitchen area and living room. Even when the weather is inclement, everyone is most likely to congregate outdoors.

And, on a late summer night—when all is quiet and the wind is just so—one can almost hear the strains of *La Traviata* wafting up toward the house from the opera below.

An old redwood harvest table creates an outdoor dining area on the portal (ABOVE LEFT). The random assortment of old chairs is in keeping with the informal theme of the outdoor spaces. The terra-cotta piece in the background is a *chimenea*, a traditional Mexican fireplace. Small amounts of wood or coal are placed in the bottom of this movable fireplace, and the heat radiates out.

Back-to-back Guatemalan hammocks hooked onto the posts of the portal offer a tranquilizing view of the northern New Mexican scenery (ABOVE).

Sculptural Beauty

Artistic Outdoor Design in Santa Fe

I N LATE WINTER in Santa Fe, the landscape glimmers and ripens toward spring. Older fruit trees often wait until past Memorial Day to blossom, seemingly in agreement with the commonly held belief of Santa Fe gardeners: No bloom is completely safe from freak blizzards until June first.

On a two-and-a-half acre homesite east of downtown Santa Fe, thousands of early blooming lemon-yellow tulips, Golden Parade, have been briefly buried in a covering of pure white snow, providing a startling juxtaposition of color and texture.

The tulips survive because the late snow disappears quickly. But the bold use of texture, scale, and color seems to be unending in this house and garden.

When the owners bought the Santa Fe acreage and a remodeled, turn-of-the-century farmhouse, they were already veteran creators of unusual houses. Ron Robles is an artisan and a "Renaissance man," designing in the various fields of architecture, interiors, sculpture, clothing, and jewelry. His father was Mexican; his mother, a native American of the Washington State Yakima tribe. He has designed houses and resorts in Los Angeles, Mexico City, and

The owners are fascinated with pre-Columbian images. They commissioned a pottery company in Mexico to copy several for them on a much larger scale than the originals. This one is found above the gate at the end of the drive (LEFT).

In the terraced gardens, an abstract metal sculpture by Ron Robles is anchored by a concrete base (ABOVE).

Hawaii as well as Santa Fe, and his unusual creative vision bears witness to his love of the tropics and for Mesoamerican cultures.

As designer of the Santa Fe house and landscapes, Robles took bold and imaginative risks. His partner, Mel Fillini, has been able to translate Robles' ideas about both the house interior and the gardens into reality.

The owners replaced the termite-ridden sections of the house in 1980, virtually creating a new structure. Though the new residence would be equally compelling in other areas of the western United States or in Mexico, the bold-scale house pays proper homage in style and materials to the prevalent Pueblo-inspired architecture of New Mexico's capital city, as well as to the architecture of the Mayans.

The private road extending several hundred yards to the house is edged with several processional landscapes. Masses of hybrid sunflowers and thousands of pink and white cosmos and white Shasta daisies border the drive; an elliptical garden planted with hundreds of roses and an old peach tree is centered in the driveway just outside the main gates to the house and garden.

After the visitor enters through large Mexican wooden gates from the drive, the sequence of plantings and other elements become more formalized. Weeping birch trees frame the entrance and enormous slabs of concrete form "stairs" leading to the house. To one side is a vast terraced garden. A wide wooden bridge serves as a transition to the concrete platform on which the new house is built, and water flows underneath the bridge from a monumental fountain—a vertical fifteen-foot rectangle of concrete, out of which an asymmetrical half-moon has been carved.

Two large concrete horses on rectangular pedestals and a witty bronze frog are among other outdoor elements, including outdoor lighting fixtures designed by Robles and Japanese garden lanterns, which add to the overall impressions of a sheltered, aesthetically pleasing outdoor space.

The sand-colored one-story adobe house rising above the terraces and gardens seems to be a monument in itself. The monolithic walls of the facade are punctuated by enormous vertical sheets of glass, equal in scale to the wooden double door in front. Through the door one enters into a space—the living room—that feels like a ceremonial center almost as large as the outdoors. Visitors are greeted by heroic statuary, copies of striking pre-Columbian figures. The interior of the main section of the house is a wide, open space, with a living room at one end, a glassed-

Shocks of pink cosmos along the drive lead into the property. The drive has become one of the best known flowerscapes among Santa Fe's gardeners (FAR TOP LEFT).

Shasta daisies and small, wild sunflowers bloom near the hills of Santa Fe in early summer. (FAR MIDDLE LEFT).

The owners built an entirely new entrance to the property, including a series of processional landscapes (FAR BOTTOM LEFT).

In early summer, irises bloom outside the rough-hewn main gate (LEFT).

51

in greenhouse room on the other, and the kitchen and dining areas in between.

Off the living room of the house is a self-contained master suite with a service kitchen and library. A guest wing, next to the main house, was remodeled around an existing structure.

The greenhouse or garden room is a tangle of lush plants and has magnificent views to the south. Elephant ear, elkhorn, and staghorn ferns are surrounded by other tropical exotica in this peaceful room. Many of the plants were brought from Hawaii and California by the owners. In winter, the room is filled with red geraniums brought indoors, which await late May when they are once again placed around the outdoor terraces.

As dramatic as the interior appears to be, it is also utilitarian, built with concrete floors and large drains, so the floors can be hosed down—an accommodation for six dogs and two cats.

Under the stewardship of the owners, the greenhouse, as well as the outdoor gardens, are among the most vibrant in Santa Fe and are often studied by others. They reintroduced cottonwood and evergreen trees that were once on the property; one of the boldest moves in the creation of the landscape took place in 1980

Simplicity and the use of natural materials give an Oriental feeling to the details in the various landscapes of the property. Rocks, a Japanese garden lantern, and a witty bronze frog add to the impeccably planned pool and fountain environment (TOP LEFT).

One of a pair of Italian concrete horses stands guard at the wide entrance of the house (BOTTOM LEFT).

Various levels of concrete "stairs" and a bridge lead to the house (ABOVE). On one side are thriving young aspen trees and a view the hills bordering Santa Fe.

in the planting of 340 aspen trees. Local nurserymen tried to discourage the owners from such a drastic step, as aspens were thought to be difficult to grow in an elevation under 7,000 feet. Yet only eleven were lost—to sap blight. The rest of the trees have grown to be twenty-five feet tall (from their seven foot planting size), and the landscape shimmers in spring and summer with silvery leaves. In autumn it seems framed in bright yellow in all directions.

The owners have entertained in the garden and on the terraces in a variety of ways. In August of most years, they hold their annual "corn party" when guests descend on the vegetable garden to the north side of the house; the corn is lush because Santa Fe is blessed with summer rain. But the owners grow many other vegetables in the garden on the west side of the house, such as lettuces, carrots, beets, squashes, and white beans as well as the more exotic white Aztec beans, similar in shape and size to lima beans.

The terraced gardens support thousands of flowers; the owners brought in thirty truckloads of dirt to replace the existing soil. The plantings include tulips, baby's breath, delphiniums, alliums, columbine, grape hyacinth, peonies, daylilies, snapdragons, irises, purple flax, coreopsis, narcissi, as well as apricot, plum, apple, cherry, and pear trees.

In this garden, neat, organized rows are not to be found. The owners plant drifts of flowers for shocks of color and texture, such as Oriental poppies, dahlias, dramatic peonies, and zinnias. In the spring, lilac bushes are in full bloom—they are a Santa Fe tradition—and add to the exquisite beauty of the landscape along the drive and on the terrace outside the guest wing. On the north side of the house, decades-old bushes bring forth masses of the fragrant white and purple blossoms.

Guests often enjoy sitting by the fountain (TOP LEFT) and the view of the aspens. In spring and summer, the leaves of the young trees shimmer silver in the sun, and in fall, turn to brilliant gold.

Lemon yellow Golden Parade tulips light up a stone wall and a collection of well-loved and well-used garden gloves and implements (LEFT).

In the dining room, the table is set for a teddy bear tea. A wolf in sheep's clothing is an unexpected guest. Beyond the scored concrete floors of the dining room is a greenhouse filled with tropical exotica—elephant ear, elkhorn, and staghorn ferns (RIGHT).

The owners pride themselves on reviving plants and trees. Ron Robles estimates that a third of their plantings were nursery throwaways, and he often shops at local nurseries in the dead of winter, when he can buy plants at bargain prices—one dollar or less for half-frozen specimens that are brought home and nursed back to health.

The house is frequented by many guests who find the gardenscapes around the property to be dramatic, a combination of flair, technology, and aesthetic balance. The owners believe a garden should be overwhelming, breathtaking—and free. "You should be able to run through a garden and not hurt anything," Ron Robles has said.

Mel Fillini works the gardens daily along with a full-time gardener. The landscapes here are a tribute to nature and man working in tandem. The trees and flowers have room to breathe and to grow, and will mark the landscape for decades to come.

On the back terrace, the
figure of a woman in the
agony of childbirth is a copy
of an ancient statue (FAR
LEFT).

A god to be reckoned with,
another copy of a pre-
Columbian image adorns the
terrace (LEFT).

On the north side of the
house, decades-old lilac
bushes bring forth masses of
the fragrant blooms
(RIGHT).

In spring, thousands of tulips dance in the clear light of the season.

The springtime terraced gardens and stone walls are ringed by aspens. This sweeping garden is at the front of the house (RIGHT).

Rocky Foothills

The Quintessential Portal Overlooking Tesuque

SOME PEOPLE drawn to life in northern New Mexico have chosen to live in one of the small, quieter communities near Santa Fe. One of these—Tesuque—might be considered one of the loveliest spots for "country" life near New Mexico's capital city.

Tesuque is only six miles north of Santa Fe in a small green valley formed by Tesuque Creek, the largest tributary of Pojoaque Creek. Tesuque is a Spanish corruption of the Tewa Indian word for "spotted dry place." The name suits it well. Outside the riparian plain of the creek where cottonwoods and willows flourish, the geology of the area is choppy in contrast to the smoother terrain of Santa Fe. The earth here is reddish, rocky, less yielding, and punctuated with ravines.

Tesuque is framed by the foothills of the southern Sangre de Cristo Range and by the Jemez Mountains, which include Redondo Peak and the basalt-capped butte known as Black Mesa, more properly known by the Pueblo Indians as Tunyo. According to legend, caves on the north side of Tunyo are the home of Tsabiyo, a monster who threatens children.

Tesuque, New Mexico, six miles north of Santa Fe, is framed by the ever- changing beauty of the foothills of the Sangre de Cristo Range and the Jemez Mountains. Here, the Hitchcock house is perched on a reddish, rocky ridge (LEFT).

The clear translucent light of late afternoon in northern New Mexico bathes one of the most dramatic portals in the region. The interior of the portal is painted Navajo white to reflect the sun (ABOVE).

The sheltered portal looks west to the Jemez Mountains and north up the Rio Grande Valley toward the Colorado border. Seventy feet long, the portal is an extension of the house, which is set dramatically into the choppy high desert (FAR LEFT).

At the north end of the portal, a garden gate leads into a patio area with raised vegetable beds and a path to the perennial garden on the east side of the house (LEFT).

The valley has been home to the Tewa Indians for almost 700 years, and the Jemez Mountains have since ancient times been a source of obsidian and chalcedony and good hunting. Although the original Tesuque Pueblo is in ruins now, the Tewas make their home in a small village located just three miles from the original pueblo.

Tesuque is also the site of one of the original Spanish towns in New Mexico. Today the Spanish town is to the east of U.S. Highway 85. The east side village has only a handful of commercial buildings—a good restaurant, a small market, and a post office. In recent years it has become a quiet enclave of special houses as well.

Eileen and Gilbert Hitchcock moved to Tesuque in 1980. The hamlet is about as far culturally and geographically from their Mies van der Rohe highrise in downtown Chicago as they could have imagined.

Gil Hitchcock has been drawn to the Southwest since he first saw it as a child, and has been a collector of Navajo blankets and pots as an adult. The couple came for a visit, spurred also by Eileen's father's opinion that Santa Fe is the most beautiful city in

America. On their second visit, they realized Santa Fe had everything they wanted—sunny days, nearby fly-fishing, art, music, and a rich cultural heritage. They decided to make the move.

The couple was sure they wanted to live near downtown Santa Fe. They could walk to work (they are both stockbrokers) as well as to restaurants, galleries, and shops. When an artist friend told them of a house high on a ridge in Tesuque in Vista Redonda, a small subdivision, the Hitchcocks were reluctant to even see it. They had considered outlying areas, but had originally decided to stay in town.

Yet, with their friend's prompting, they did go to see the simple, New Mexican adobe house with its stark desert setting and views of the ever-changing skies of New Mexico. They purchased the house the next day.

The roughly Y-shaped earth-colored adobe house took three years to build in the early 1970s. Its long and narrow shape was determined by the hilltop: where the ridge widens out, so does the house. The adobe residence has a modest, understated entrance and a flat roof. The interior is organized around traditional lines, with a kitchen at one end of the house and at the

65

Beyond the stepped wall of the portal, two apple trees and a Montmorency cherry share space on the south patio with contemporary sculpture (RIGHT).

A study in contrasting materials, shapes, and color at the intersection of the portal and sun room. The freestanding metal sculpture is *Flume* by Santa Fe artist Tom Waldron (MIDDLE RIGHT).

In the perennial garden, a sculpture cut in steel by Santa Fe artist Bob Haozous reveals a feline's wild nature (FAR RIGHT).

other, a bedroom wing. The two areas are bridged by dining and living rooms.

As charming as the house appeared to the couple, its setting proved to be the most compelling element in their decision to move to Tesuque. The ridgetop has sweeping views of the high desert to the west, north, and south. The silence and solitude of the desert welcomed them.

They went to work immediately on the house. On the interior, they replaced doors, painted much of the woodwork, built bookcases, tiled the kitchen, and extended two partial kitchen walls nearly to the ceiling. Additional remodeling took place outdoors.

The new owners built high garden walls on the east and south sides of the house, which are punctuated by inset, abstract sculptures of copper and bronze designed by area Santa Fe sculptor Vignir Johannsson.

The Hitchcocks then constructed an adobe and glass sun room to the south of the kitchen where there had been a small portal. The sun room is used in winter and is furnished with comfortable wicker chairs, a chaise, and a table. The new owners linger here with coffee on weekend mornings, enjoying the brilliant winter sun of northern New Mexico. It is also a garden room where the couple bring in geraniums and other potted flowers to shield them from cold winter weather. This room is extended by an outdoor patio accessible by French doors. The patio is set with two freestanding contemporary sculptures, *Walking Man* by John Connell and *Flume* by Tom Waldron.

At the front of the house, the owners remodeled an existing storage shed into an office. The most elaborate planning for their new residence, however, was for a portal running the length of the west side of the house, in full view of the Jemez Mountains,

which was to be seventy feet long and thirteen feet deep. When it was constructed, the Hitchcocks had added an entirely new physical and aesthetic dimension to the existing house. The portal became a true extension of the house into the desert and onto the rocky ridge itself. It is the portal that allows the couple the luxury of living outdoors protected from the sun during the day and from cold in the evenings, and allows for spectacular, almost uninterrupted views of the high desert to the west and north.

The portal is a contemporary interpretation of the traditional New Mexican form. Its pillars are topped with carved corbels and protruding *canales* (drain spouts), and underneath each canale, on the ground, is an orderly row of stone metates (used by Southwestern Indians for the grinding of corn) to direct water draining from the roof into the garden directly in front of the portal. Pots of geraniums are placed between the pillars in season.

A corner fireplace was designed to be both grill and fireplace, allowing the couple to cook outdoors and serve directly onto the portal's rectangular dining table.

The exterior walls of the house that form the back of the portal are stuccoed in Navajo white—an off-white color that lightens the interior of the portal.

The most striking area of visual interest on the portal, however, is a wooden menagerie—the Hitchcock's collection of large-scale whimsical contemporary folk art animals. Santa Fe has had a boom in recent years in the tongue-in-cheek, brightly painted animals, and the owners' beasts are among the best. Most of their animals were carved by disciples of sculptor Felipe Archuleta. The tiger and camel were carved by Leroy Archuleta, the gray elephant by Leroy Ortega, and the bear by Alonso Jimenez, who also carved the witty crocodile and a friendly pig.

Folk artist Monica Halford painted the *retablo* (a painting of a religious subject on wood) of saints Peter and Paul, which has a place of honor on the wall above the couch on the portal. The owners commissioned her to paint bucolic scenes on interior doors as well.

The portal is an extension of the house, and for several months of the year it is where the owners dine, relax, and entertain. They most often have small dinner parties and Sunday brunches here, using the outdoor grill for simple but well-thought-out meals of lamb, duck, steak, or chicken and late Sunday morning breakfasts of French toast, eggs, or crepes. The portal is also the heart of larger dinner and cocktail parties for as many as eighty guests. The couple especially enjoy entertaining in June, when nights on their ridge are the warmest.

Northern New Mexico has worked its magic on the Hitchcocks. They have become not only collectors of contemporary New Mexican folk art, but also of early twentieth-century paintings from the Santa Fe and Taos schools. Gil Hitchcock has fallen in love with twentieth-century photography. He is now well versed on the subject, and collects prints of the most prominent photographers, including those of Paul Caponigro, William Clift, and Eliot Porter. But the most remarkable transformation has been that of Eileen Hitchcock from city dweller to country gardener.

She grew up on Long Island, New York, and spent most of her adult life in Chicago. The wide open spaces and rich landscapes of New Mexico sparked her interest in gardening. She observed the gardens of Santa Fe, and wondered why so many people landscaped with what appeared to be weeds; she also read extensively, and began an eight-year apprenticeship as desert gardener during their first spring in the house. She remembers buying a flat of the flowering plant, snow-in-summer. She brought them home and hacked out little holes in the hard, miserable ground. A few plants actually lived.

Soft shadows play across the screened doors of the sun-room (LEFT), where the owners breakfast and enjoy the brilliant winter sun of northern New Mexico.

A traditional Pueblo ladder leans against a wall where adobe meets stone (RIGHT).

An antique, weathered cart finds a new use in the perennial garden on the east side of the house (BELOW).

The honeyed light of late afternoon falls upon the dining table on the portal, fully dressed for an evening meal. After grilling outdoors for dinner, the owners will light a piñon wood fire to warm themselves on their ridgetop.

The delicately shaded gray elephant carved by Leroy Ortega is an important member of the owners' folk art menagerie (TOP RIGHT).

Leroy Archuleta's tongue-in-cheek, wonderfully patterned tiger stands guard by the door leading from the portal into the living room (MIDDLE RIGHT).

The friendly desert camel is the creation of wood-carver Leroy Archuleta (BOTTOM RIGHT).

Eileen Hitchcock continued her gardening through eight years of trial and error. Tesuque's ridgetops are composed of rocky, heavy clay soil in which she had to use a pick. The soil was also alkaline, but workable if enough humus was added to it. If anything she planted didn't perform in a year, out it went. She discovered many plants that liked alkaline soil, and she discovered, too, the gardener's joy of accomplishment.

The result of her apprenticeship can now be seen in a variety of gardenscapes. The "rough" garden set with large rocks in front of the portal is a xeriscape, planted with drought-resistant ornamentals. Eileen Hitchcock wanted this garden to resemble the natural desert, for it is the window through which the couple look at the untrammeled valley below their property. It has also been planted with plants that bear blue flowers, with the exception of the tall, alkaline-loving chamisa that brings forth dense, gold-yellow clusters of feathery flowers in late August, lasting through September.

This garden was a real challenge to the new gardener and was replanted five times. Besides the chamisa, silvery Russian sage, which blooms pale blue to deep violet, lavender, catmint, salvia, four varieties of campanula (bellflower), and silvery green desert sage, a relative of the chamisa, have been among the survivors of the native garden.

On the east side of the house the couple enclosed with a wall what was basically a wasted no-man's-land. The stony dirt here was removed and replaced with richer, finer soil for the creation of a classic perennial garden. Creeping thyme is planted in between the steps of a flagstone walkway, which bisects rich beds of daylilies, lavender, saponaria, tall campanula, lythrum, coreopsis, Shasta daisies, malva, and trollius, among other plants—including English and Boston ivy—all chosen for their hardiness. Two apple trees, a Bradford pear, and several ornamental plums give the garden structure and shade.

Among the sculpture on the south patio, Gil Hitchcock has planted two more apple trees and a Montmorency cherry.

The views from the portal of the Jemez Mountains and the mesas of the Rio Grande Valley are awe-inspiring to the homeowners, just as they have been to the people of this land since ancient times. The owners have a clear view of Redondo Peak, which is sacred to the Pueblo Indians. The 11,000-foot peak had a shrine on the eastern side of its summit. It was visited each year in August by Pueblo groups until the early part of this century. Its magic remains.

Pueblo Meadows

A Cottage Garden in the Lush Valley of Taos

Taos, New Mexico looks very much like a sagebrush prairie. Yet the climate there is such that the earth warms slowly in early summer and cools off quickly once summer has ended—weather that is more fitting for what Taos really is—the opening to the Rocky Mountains. The Sangre de Cristo Range, a splinter of the Rockies, dominates Taos to the east and slices through the earth more than 100 miles into Colorado.

This striking, high land was first settled by the Taos Indians in the late fourteenth or early fifteenth century. The mud masonry, multistoried Taos Pueblo is still their home. The pueblo is four miles outside the town of Taos, which was founded by the Spanish in 1610. Anglo-Americans have been attracted to this Spanish and Pueblo Indian community and its wild beauty since the 1850s. Artists and writers came to stay in the early years of the twentieth century, and Taos has long had the reputation of enfolding creative, independent, and hard-working people within its rich valley and lush green meadows.

In 1979 Ranna Wiswall, a gold and silversmith, arrived in Taos from her New England upbringing and education. She first supported herself and her

Purple clematis winds its way around the high willow arch of the garden gate, while blue flax stands sentinel outside the garden. The pale, creamy yellow blooms of potentilla, a Southwestern shrub, flourish hardily through the summer.

A carved granite birdbath by Taos stonemason Miles Sintetos is bordered by white perennials (ABOVE).

Twisted columns painted a Taos turquoise add a bit of Spanish Colonial kitsch to the *sombra* (an outdoor, shaded room), which is furnished with the joyful painted furniture of Taos artisan Jim Wagner (LEFT). Aspen *latillas* (saplings) spaced four inches apart form the "roof" of the sombra to allow both light and shade.

Clumps of vibrant daylilies in the high-altitude garden are a tribute to the owners' love of flowers and color. (RIGHT).

toddler son by plying her trade in Taos, making handmade silver jewelry. Wiswall soon became enchanted with the 700-year adobe building traditions in Taos. Many houses in Taos continue to be built in the old ways, by hand and with mud. Wiswall, by hard work and assiduous study, followed the footsteps of Spanish women who settled in New Mexico centuries before her. She became an *enjarradora*—adobe mud plasterer. Wiswall learned how to prepare the color slip variations used for plastering adobe walls from the earth itself, in colors ranging from mauve to ocher to oyster white. She also learned how to sculpt in mud, creating traditional *fogons* (corner fireplaces), *nichos*, (wall niches), and *bancos* (benches).

While working on a Taos adobe in 1982, she met Jeremiah Buchanan, an adobe builder and gardener. The two soon mar-

ried, and in 1984, the parents of two small children and Ranna's six-year-old son, they began building an adobe house of their own on a two-acre site.

Located at an elevation of 7,100 feet in the El Tros area of Taos, their homesite is just below Talpa Ridge. Above them is national forest land, and trails near their property lead up the mountain.

The couple share strongly held beliefs about living off the land and protection and conservation of the environment. It was their intention to build a house and plant an organic vegetable garden that would allow them self-sufficiency. Ranna Wiswall grew up watching her father garden; plants became her first love. The garden plan included planting flowers along with vegetables on a quarter-acre adjacent to their new house.

The couple began working on their homesite by removing sagebrush by hand, as they agreed bulldozing the site would strip it of precious topsoil. Jeremiah Buchanan excavated the site for the cement footings by hand, laid up the adobe bricks himself, and with some assistance hoisted up the *vigas*—peeled spruce logs—which form the foundation of the roof.

The traditional earth-colored Pueblo-style adobe house took shape slowly. The south-facing rectangular house was built on a slant, following the lay of the land. Its four-level tin roof is surrounded by a stepped parapet wall echoing the design of the Taos Pueblo.

The interior of the house has a large central room with an open kitchen. To the east of the central room are three bedrooms. On the opposite side of the main room is a greenhouse where the owners cultivate orchids, ferns, and Jeremiah Buchanan's passions—succulents and cacti. At the lowest level of the house is a meditation room that doubles as a guest room.

The residence is mud-plastered inside and out. The interior plastering especially reflects the enjarradora skills of Ranna Wiswall and her partners, Jennifer and Donna Brown. The main room of the house is pale beige, known as *tierra vallita*. In the master bedroom pink sand was mixed with mud to give a rosy glow to the finish. The children's bedrooms are *tierra blanca*—white earth, and the master bedroom and bath have stenciled borders based on Native American geometric designs of red slip mixed with mica, which gives a slight luminescence to the medium.

The outdoor rooms and garden have been designed so that every detail facilitates the owners' desires to create beauty along with sustenance for the family. A north-facing adobe courtyard with an arched entrance and willow gate is used by Ranna Wiswall for plants needing moisture and protection—daylilies, white coralbells, primroses, wisteria, peonies, geraniums, campanula, and feathery white and pink astilbe. In winter this courtyard has been covered with five feet of drifting snow. In summer orchids and cacti from the greenhouse are brought here. At other times of the year, the courtyard plant beds are kept moist because the roof was designed to drain to the north side of the house.

The most recent addition to the outdoor area is an open room with flagstone flooring facing the garden. The owners call this room a *sombra*, meaning "shade" in Spanish. Its roof is constructed of aspen *latillas* (saplings) spaced four inches apart to

A view of the arched courtyard entrance on the north side of the house is framed by the ever-present sagebrush of Taos (LEFT).

The mud-plastered adobe house was inspired by the stepped planes of the 700-year-old Taos Pueblo. One of the owners, an *enjarradora* (mud plasterer) by trade, was assisted in the plastering of the house by two partners. The protruding spruce log vigas form the foundation of the roof and were hoisted into place by the owners (TOP RIGHT).

The family cat nestles against the latillas of a courtyard window (BOTTOM RIGHT).

Young willows were collected from the banks of the Rio Grande by the owners to form the arched gate leading into the half-moon-shaped garden (FAR TOP LEFT).

Along the western perimeter of the garden, purple delphiniums reach up the aspen latilla fence (TOP LEFT).

Daylilies and white valerian grow near the stone steps leading to the garden's S-shaped pathway (FAR BOTTOM LEFT). The owners grow scores of other herbs used for cooking and medicinal purposes.

Purple coneflowers (*Echinacea*) and coronation gold yarrow beneath the Talpa Ridge (BOTTOM LEFT).

Pink cosmos with its lacy and delicate foliage (RIGHT) adds grace and beauty to summer tables.

allow for light and for shade. The southern side of the sombra is completely open, and its western side is a half-wall and banco allowing for views of the garden. The other two sides of the sombra are formed by another banco and a wall of the greenhouse. The owners furnish the room in summer with brightly painted furniture made by Taos craftsman Jim Wagner.

In planning the life-giving garden, which is becoming well known in Taos, the couple thought out each component of the soil. They began preparing their garden as soon as their well was dug. Jeremiah Buchanan has a long-time interest in soils and soil preparation. They helped their high-altitude soil first by bringing in loads of sand from nearby arroyos to lighten its high clay content, and second by adding organic compost, which adds mi-

croorganisms to enliven the soil and to help plants to absorb nutrients. They also added granular kelp and other kelp-based products containing sixty trace minerals along with natural growth hormones. Colloidal phosphate from ground rocks provides phosphate, lacking in heavy clay soils.

The garden is terraced to collect water draining from the Talpa Ridge above the property, and it is mulched to hold the water, reflecting the owners' belief in water conservation. The organic soil in their garden is like a sponge, and has been described by a neighbor as "good enough to eat." The owners believe soil is alive and work continuously at its cultivation. Their experience in soil preparation eventually led them to form a company, El Tros. The couple now restore adobe soils for a living.

Against a threatening summer sky, award-winning corn thrives in the short summer growing season in Taos (FAR TOP LEFT). The family often enters their produce in local fairs.

Organically fed chickens supply the family with fresh eggs year round (TOP LEFT).

Regal red hollyhocks reach to a double-hung window on the board and batten workshop/garage near the east side of the house (FAR BOTTOM LEFT).

Tall Kentucky Wonder beans will climb these tied aspen poles (BOTTOM LEFT).

The owners refer to their half-moon-shaped cultivated land as a "cottage" garden; its natural, relaxed form dates from the mid-nineteenth century in England and Holland. The Wiswall-Buchanan garden is entered by a willow archway and gate (the willows were collected by the couple from the banks of the Rio Grande), which is covered with purple clematis. The ground around the gate is planted potentilla shrubs, which bloom with pale yellow roselike flowers. Curving paths sweep through the planting beds and are bordered with redwood bender boards and crushed rock. Low stone walls encircle the garden north to south, and its western perimeter is marked by an aspen pole fence.

Flowers, vegetables, herbs, and shrubs are planted together in this "wild" garden. In the center is a ring of irises and rich, velvety snapdragons, along with potentilla, chard, and spinach. There are salvias in the carrots, and some paths are lined with early-blooming miniature Shasta daisies and others with chives. The sometimes planned, sometimes serendipitous arrangement has brought forth its own ecosystem. The garden has never had a serious insect infestation, and the flowers attract butterflies and birds—red-wing blackbirds, two species of hummingbirds, a rare mountain bluebird as well as magpies, sparrows, ravens, finches, and jays. Martins call at sunrise and sunset, and after dark, nighthawks visit.

Ranna Wiswall loves flowers. She is determined to have every variety she can, and each year adds to her collection of perennials and annuals. She orders seeds and bulbs from all over the world—Europe, Africa, and Australia—and she is trying to collect every type of sun-loving perennial that can be planted in ordinary soil. She is as intrigued with plant biology as she is with beautiful flowers, and keeps a filing system of plants and flowers, in the garden, noting species, family, planting conditions, and progress. Wiswall especially likes shrub roses, and grows them from seeds. She has started an Alpine garden, using gritty, rocky soil, and has planted a garden of native Southwestern plants—varieties of penstemon (beard tongue), yarrows, Indian paint brush, as well as sunflowers and potentilla.

Wiswall searches catalogs for unusual annuals, and she is especially interested in color. The entire outer crescent of the garden is planted with yellow, red, and orange flowers, interspersed with flowering plants in other colors combined with yellow. There is a perennial blue garden—tinged with purples and pinks and reds—of veronicas, liatris, delphiniums, phlox, and campanulas.

Plum purple jackmanii
clematis glows in the
morning sun (RIGHT).

The seeds from several
varieties of Russian giant
sunflowers are part of the
garden's annual bounty
(FAR TOP RIGHT).

Delicate orange California
poppies bloom in summer
and reseed themselves
every year (FAR BOTTOM
RIGHT).

The couple have a strong belief in open-pollinated vegetables and have planted them wherever possible. Taos has a remarkably short growing season—about 100 days—and the amount and variety of vegetables grown by the owners is daunting. Among their cold weather crops are red and shamrock cabbage, kohlrabi, broccoli, white Voss cauliflower from France, and four varieties of onions—the two sweet types are grown from seeds. They harvest varieties of carrots, beets, spinach, tomatoes, peppers, and lettuces, along with three types of corn (one of which won Jeremiah Buchanan Best Corn at the Taos County Fair), five varieties of peas, and beans.

In summer, the family enjoys two varieties of watermelon, cantaloupe, strawberries, and four types of summer squash, and in the fall, pumpkin. They make their own vinegar with herbs grown in the garden, and store much of their potato crop for the winter. Wiswall puts up vegetables that are used all winter long—winter squash and pumpkins, among others. She freezes corn on and off the cob, along with chard and lamb's quarters, a delicious weed rather like a cross between lettuce and chard. They feast, too, on raspberries and strawberries, as well as fruit from orchard trees—plums, peaches, sour cherries, apricots, and apples.

The owners keep chickens and are supplied year-round with fertilized eggs. The chickens are fed table scraps and their droppings are added to the compost pile kept beyond the back fence. In the same area is a plant and tree nursery with plum trees, Russian olives, apple trees, and hackberries.

This garden unfolds its glories month by month, from April to October. Purple chive and Shasta daisies bloom early. In late June, hundreds of lilies—yellows, oranges, reds, whites, and pinks show themselves. By early October, the last of the vegetables are harvested, and the asters and chrysanthemums are still holding on.

The owners are constantly working to improve gardening techniques and crop yield. With their handmade house and fruitful garden to sustain them, they feel in control of their lives and have set an example for others. One of their greatest joys is to be told that yet another friend is about to try planting a high-altitude organic garden.

Mesa Magic

A Gracious Garden for an Updated Adobe Near Taos

MOST VISITORS approach Taos from the south, coming from the more populous areas of Santa Fe or Albuquerque. The drive is through the dramatic Rio Grande Canyon, where one's attention is captivated by the magnificent, rushing river. Eventually the road climbs and the narrow confines of the gorge give way to the wide-open plateau upon which the town of Taos is situated. The backdrop of this culturally rich community is the dramatic peaks of the Sangre de Cristo Mountains.

On the outskirts of Taos, an unassuming dirt road winds through high mesa scrub. Flanking either side of the road are vast stretches of *chamisa*, or golden rabbitbrush, a shrub that changes from silver-green to golden as summer progresses into autumn. At the far end of the road, a magnificent stand of mountain cottonwoods becomes visible, which, in the topographical language of the Southwest, signals a residence protected by shade.

Beneath the shady boughs of the cottonwoods and behind the plump, golden-peach adobe garden walls, sits a gracious Pueblo-style house. The rambling house, also made of adobe, is T-shaped and is surrounded by flower-

As seen from the side, the pool house (LEFT) has its own small portal, simply furnished with *equipale* or Mexican pigskin furniture.

Old-fashioned hollyhocks (ABOVE) do well in Taos's high elevation; they add height to the front yard's flowerbeds.

Set on a stretch of sage and chamisa, the adobe house is shaded by a tall stand of cottonwood trees. Most of the property's twenty seven acres have been left in a natural state; the more formal gardens surround the house.

The Houstons use the front courtyard (ABOVE) to serve welcoming cocktails or to have intimate outdoor dinners. A barbecue is built into the low wall at left. The portal, or covered porch, runs the length of the front of the house and is a protective spot for groupings of rustic furniture. The wooden ladder is a traditional New Mexican piece. In the flowerbeds, yellow and purple pansies and pink geraniums provide a splash of color in the foreground. White impatiens are used in the tree wells and in the hanging baskets.

beds and pots filled with blossoms of subtle and brilliant hues. In the front, there's a welcoming courtyard with a cool portal, or covered porch, which runs along the exterior of the residence. To one side of the house, a swimming pool is a refreshing sight; on the opposite side, a wild flower meadow is a gentle contrast to the magnificently landscaped grounds. And in the back, the yard is dominated by the tall trees.

However, neither the house nor the flower-filled grounds were in any great condition when the owners, Ruth and George Houston, first saw the property in the mid-1970s. In fact, the house at that time was a restaurant.

George Houston had recently taken over his family's lumber business based in Kansas, and whatever free time the Houstons had, they spent vacationing in Taos. Eventually, the magic of Taos, its artistic community, and its Spanish and Indian origins captivated the Houstons, and they began to house-hunt.

"We wanted a big, old adobe," says Ruth Houston, "and they're hard to come by, let alone find in good shape." After some searching, they found this house, which had been originally a grain mill in the mid-nineteenth century, then a private residence. As is the tradition with older adobe houses of the Southwest, rooms were added to this one over the decades as the

families who lived there grew larger. Then it became an outdoor restaurant, with the tall, graceful cottonwoods adding drama to the ambience.

The Houstons began remodeling the house not long after they acquired the property. Working with architect William Lumpkins of Santa Fe, they reorganized the interior spaces to provide views of the outdoors and to accommodate their frequent houseguests. A master suite was also added. The new construction was done in adobe as well, its architectural style blending discreetly with the hand-plastered, rounded forms of the Pueblo motif of the older parts of the house.

For the inside, the Houstons utilized the talents of Donald Random Murphy, an interior designer from Santa Fe, to help with the selection of furnishings, colors, accessories, and art. Murphy mixed Southwestern and Mexican antiques and contemporary pieces to create a setting that complements the rustic architecture yet also manages to convey a subtle sense of tradition and formality.

Although Taos' summer season is relatively short (at an elevation of 7,000 feet, Taos is at the southern tip of the Rocky Mountains and has a cool climate), the Houstons knew that they wanted to take full advantage of the sun-drenched summer days by focusing attention on the exterior of their house. Though they had a total of twenty-seven acres with which to work, they opted to develop only the three acres surrounding the house and to leave the remaining land in its natural state of meadow and brush.

They worked with several landscape designers over the course of the years to come up with a range of inviting spots for dining, entertaining, and relaxing, all highlighted by the beauty and fragrance of the garden flowers.

When the Houstons first purchased the house, a gravel driveway and parking lot came right up to the front entry. This was replaced with lawn, brick-paved walkways, and flowerbeds, and an inviting front courtyard was created. This manicured courtyard is separated from the meadows and wild scrub beyond by an undulating adobe garden wall.

Within this front courtyard, which is entered through a weathered, antique Mexican gate, the brick walkway leads toward a larger brick-paved patio, complete with a barbecue area, and the front portal, where the Houstons often greet arriving guests. The courtyard is surrounded by two main wings of the house (one comprising the kitchen, living and dining rooms,

and the master suite; the other containing George Houston's office and the guest bedrooms), and many of the rooms in these wings have doors that open onto the courtyard.

To one side of the exterior the Houstons added more pathways and a small patio just off the master bedroom. This quiet space affords a view of the distant mountains and is a pleasant spot to read the morning paper.

Just a bit beyond this patio is the new pool, which is an irregular, lagoon shape, and a spa. The pool's flagstone decking is inset with several large rocks that provide whimsical seating areas in addition to the pool furniture. Pots of flowers surround the pool and spa area, and from the comfortable vantage point of the spa, one is able to view the beautiful surrounding wild flower meadow. The pool house, built to architecturally complement the main house, contains storage space, changing rooms, and a bar, done in a cantina theme, and has doors that can be thrown open toward the pool's flagstone patio areas.

When the Houstons bought the house, the backyard had the cottonwoods, a generous expanse of lawn, and an *acequia*, or a small irrigation canal, that cut through the property—and they decided to leave much of it as it was. On this side of the house, though, they added another portal and a new barbecue. Because this portal is adjacent to the dining and living rooms, it is frequently used for al fresco lunches and dinners. Nearby, there is a fire pit surrounded by a circular *banco*, or bench, which can easily seat an informal dinner gathering.

Along the wing opposite the master suite, each guest room—and the office—has a private patio area that overlooks the wild flower meadow.

The Houstons also worked with Donald Murphy to appropriately furnish the "exterior rooms"—the portals, or porches, and patios. Rustic Mexican and New Mexican antiques are used closer to the house where they are protected from the elements; dining tables, chairs, benches, and chests are arranged to provide inviting settings in which to dine, visit, read, and so forth. Antique artifacts, imported pottery, outdoor murals, and red chile *ristras*, or strands, were carefully chosen to give the spaces a well-appointed look. In some of the patio areas is *equipale*, or pigskin furniture made in Mexico, and coupled with canvas and wood umbrellas, this provides a classic Southwestern complement

A low, curving wall leads up
the steps from the pool
house toward the pool and
spa. The large terra-cotta
pots hold annuals such as
marigolds, petunias, and
morning glories. The market
umbrella is by Santa
Barbara Designs.

for the adobe Pueblo-style exterior. Near the pool and in other open areas are attractive cushioned redwood chaises and rust-finish metal furniture.

Much of the sheer pleasure of being outdoors at the Houston's, however, is derived from the fragrant flowerbeds and flowerpots, which provide splashes of color that contrast vividly with the green of the lawns and trees and the golden-peach adobe walls of the house. The flowers, as well as the compact vegetable garden, are a labor of love for both gardener Rick Klein and Ruth Houston. Over the years, detailed notes have been kept on the garden's various successes and failures; at any given time, some of the plantings are experiments to see how they fare in Taos' soil and climatic conditions.

In the front courtyard, Ruth Houston wanted a more formal look, so they mixed a variety of annuals and perennials such as delphiniums, geraniums, Shasta daisies, hollyhocks, baby's breath, dahlias, violas, gladioli, and marigolds in the gently curving beds, pots, and tree wells around the stately elms. Wisteria hangs over the front gate, and a rosebush that may well date back to the time of the Spanish settlers dominates one of the courtyard's beds.

Near the pool and on the back portal are dozens of pots with more annuals: Morning glories, alyssum, petunias, and impatiens provide color and fragrance. Not far from the back portal, just outside the kitchen, a vegetable garden (broccoli, cauliflower, herbs, onions, lettuces, and chard) and a cutting garden have been cultivated and supply vegetables and fresh flowers.

Over the years, as the Houstons have become more familiar with their New Mexican surroundings, the garden has also become filled with more native species. A wild flower meadow is being nurtured near the guest wing. On what was once construction rubble left over from the remodeling, the subtle blooms of summer and early fall have been coaxed to take root. Blue flax, wild grasses, fire wheel, penstemon, and prairie coneflowers dot the meadow and have found their way into some of the peripheral flowerbeds, serving to soften the transition between the formal areas of the yard and the untamed sections of the Houston's property. Wild flower seeds are harvested in the autumn; then the spent flowers are mowed down and reseeded in the spring.

Work on the garden begins in April and continues through November, when the flowerpots are emptied and stored. Frosts come as late as June and as early as September, and in between,

Outdoor meals are frequently enjoyed during the summer months on the back portal (RIGHT). A weathered wooden table and handcrafted chairs are enhanced by Mexican pottery plates and a centerpiece of red impatiens. Red chile *ristras*, or strands, and a mural by Santa Fe artist David Scott Melville add further interest to the portal.

Behind the folding doors, a cozy bar with a cantina theme takes up most of the pool house (TOP MIDDLE RIGHT). Interior designer Donald Murphy had the traditional *equipale*, or Mexican pigskin furniture, painted white to brighten the space. The light fixture is from Mexico. The other portion of the pool house contains changing rooms and storage.

In the backyard, a fire pit is encircled by a *banco*, or bench, the site of many informal dinners (FAR TOP RIGHT). Southwestern cushions and blankets are brought outdoors as the occasion—and temperatures—warrant.

Shasta daisies, Spanish bluebells, and cosmos line a garden path (BOTTOM MIDDLE RIGHT).

Equipale, and a Santa Barbara Designs market umbrella provide a pleasing spot on the patio behind the guest wing of the house (FAR BOTTOM RIGHT). Banks of brightly hued petunias and Mexican terra-cotta pots filled with alyssum and geraniums lure houseguests out from their quarters.

thunderstorms and hail can wreak havoc on the flowers. The property has an automatic spray system for watering the lawns and flowerbeds, drip irrigation for the younger trees. The flowerpots are watered by hand, and organic fertilizers are used to feed the plantings.

The magnificent cottonwoods are George Houston's bailiwick. He believes that they may be more than a century old and pampers them to ensure another century of growth. The trees are pruned regularly, sprayed for disease, and deep-root fertilized.

He had lightning rods wired into the trees to deflect the bolts during the frequent New Mexican thunderstorms.

The cottonwoods and the rest of the landscape have provided a magnificent backdrop from which the Houstons can enjoy the clear air and crystalline light of their northern New Mexico house. If they are alone, they frequently find themselves dining outdoors, reading in a shady spot, or enjoying the sun by the pool. They enjoy hosting luncheon parties (nights can be a bit nippy, even in the summer), setting up a buffet on the back por-

The early morning rays light up the back of the house and the trunks of the mountain cottonwoods. The twenty-nine cottonwoods on the property are thought to be more than 100 years old and stand as high as 125 feet. The trees are pruned regularly and have lightning rods attached to them to deflect the bolts during the frequent summer thunderstorms.

tal and spreading out tables on the lawn under the trees. The Houstons have had as many as 150 people at the house for a party, using the indoor bar (luckily situated just off the back portal) and the bar in the pool house simultaneously. The layout of the house, both interior and exterior, works perfectly for a large crowd.

Even though the warm season is short, the Houstons find themselves enjoying their landscape year-round. In the autumn, the leaves on the cottonwoods turn golden, and the play of light on the chamisa and sage in the outlying areas is breathtaking. By winter, the flowerpots have been emptied and stored, as have some of the outdoor furnishings. Nonetheless, Ruth Houston notes that it is one of her favorite times of the year. The sun shines often during the colder months. "The snow plays up against the tree trunks, and its contrast with the red chile ristras is just gorgeous," she says. "We light *farolitos* [traditional Southwestern lanterns made of candles placed inside brown paper bags] outdoors at night, and everything is so cozy."

The first of Arizona's gardens—forest clearings, valleys, and riverbanks—were discovered, not made, by the state's earliest people. Yet these very places are as different from one another in climate and character as California's Death Valley is from the mountains of Alaska.

In the northern climes of the state, where the Colorado Plateau enters Arizona from beyond its boundaries, are Arizona's highest mountains, the San Francisco Peaks. Here on the plateau, the Colorado River has cut through time to create the Grand Canyon—a vast stone layer cake, each rich stratum nourishing the understanding of man about the formation of the earth.

Farther to the east live the Hopi and Navajo people, descendants of prehistoric hunters and gatherers. Theirs is a harsh, unforgiving climate of spectacular beauty where tribes farm and tend flocks as their ancestors did. This is the land of Monument Valley, and of ancient Anasazi ruins nestled in sandstone layered atop purple-red rock.

The Colorado Plateau spreads through one-third of the state, and its elevation varies as much as 10,000 feet. There are areas of desert grasslands, sagebrush, pygmy forests of Ponderosa pine, and, at the higher elevations, spruce, firs, and aspens—these are the biotic zones, which attract human desert dwellers by the thousands to their cooler temperatures each summer.

The dry, harsh Sonoran Desert makes up another third of the state. Within it, Arizona's two major urban areas contain most of the state's four million people. The populace sustains itself in the desert with ingenuity and engineering—just as it did almost two thousand years ago.

The story of the people and the land of southern Arizona is keyed around the one crucial life-sustaining element—water. The Hohokam were the first to harness rivers for their own use. They settled around 200 B.C. in the Salt River Valley, where Phoenix is now located, as well as 120 miles to the southeast in the Santa Cruz River Valley, where Tucson emerged centuries later.

Although the river valleys were rich, the desert was dry and unsuitable for agriculture. The Hohokam became skilled farmers and hydraulic engineers, digging a system of canals to bring water from the Salt and Santa Cruz rivers to their fields of maize, beans, squash, tobacco, and cotton. Though most of their villages were built along these watercourses, others farther away were equipped with water-gathering ditches to collect the precious substance from surface runoff. The ancient people seemed to live in concert with the natural desert as well, using native plants for food and medicine.

The Hohokam abandoned the river valleys around A.D. 1400. Their descendants, the Papago and Pima Indians, emerged around 1700 and lived peaceful, agricultural lives.

In the late seventeenth century, gardens of the Spanish missions in the Santa Cruz Valley were bringing forth the fruits of the Old World—melons, figs, dates, pomegranates, citrus, and olives. California fan palms, pepper trees, and other ornamentals were giving shade and succor to the padres, too—the first ornamentals to grace the gardens of the New World. The missionaries also cultivated the delicate blooms of the hollyhock, carnation, nasturtium, Castilian rose, canna lily, jonquil, and violet behind the cloistered walls of the missions in what was then called New Spain.

The missions didn't quite make it to the Salt River Valley. It wasn't until Anglo-Americans looking to make their fortunes in the late 1860s arrived that the desert began to sustain yet another growing population. Yet the problem of water again had to be solved. In 1867 the first irrigation ditch since the time of the Hohokam snaked its way through the valley.

This ditch sparked an agricultural revolution and spawned other irrigation canals. By the end of the century, thousands of acres of alfalfa, wheat, barley, and corn were under cultivation. Impressed with the blooming desert, pioneers built houses and landscaped them with thirsty nonindigenous trees and lawns.

A terrible drought in the late 1890s dried up the Salt River and sent many farmers and homesteaders fleeing to more hospitable climes. But the federal 1902 Reclamation Act eventually brought hope to the Salt River Valley and the rest of the Arizona Territory. Water reservoirs were financed and built by the tenets of the new law, and the federal government bought the valley's private canals and organized them into one system.

With the completion of the Roosevelt Dam eighty miles east of Phoenix in 1911, the greening of the desert rolled along at breakneck speed. Citrus, date, and olive groves were added to other crops, and Phoenix was planted with fig, ash, pecan, maple, and eucalyptus along with scores of other trees and plants never intended for the desert. The core of Phoenix, thanks to water engineering, was really no longer a desert at all.

At the end of the nineteenth century, Tucson, too, experienced an influx of Anglo-Americans, and they continued the tradition of the plants and trees introduced more than a century earlier in mission gardens. New settlers also brought date palms along with eucalyptus, Lady Banks' roses, and canna lilies, now all quite common in Tucson.

Both Tucson and Phoenix came into their own as cities during the 1920s when the first subdivisions were built. This was the era of the bungalow, and the small lots on which they stood were planted typically with pyracantha, pittosporum, roses, citrus trees, palms, and junipers.

In this era, Arizona developed resorts and dude ranches, which were to impress upon the imagination of the rest of the country an image of what Arizona was all about—desert and the Wild West. The Tanque Verde Ranch, now a century old, at the edge of Saguaro National Monument near Tucson, for example, and the now-destroyed Jokake Inn of Phoenix served as examples of how to live and play in a more or less natural desert environment. Ironically, sixty years or more after they were created, these landscapes would serve as models for designers and architects trying to reestablish the use of native plants in their natural habitat.

The greatest boom in both cities came with the post-war era and the perfection of air-conditioning. Both cities quickly grew away from their central cores into the deserts, where bulldozers, for the most part, stripped away natural vegetation and "proper" landscaping was installed.

The populations of the two urban areas within the Sonoran Desert continually grow. People are seeking the good life here—hiking, climbing, bicycle riding, golf, swimming, boating on man-made lakes (part of the vast system of water storage and flood control near Phoenix)—and are living an outdoor life in their backyards, even in summer, when temperatures climb to 110 degrees and seem to stay there for an eternity.

Tucson, with its twelve-inch annual precipitation, grew up to be a city of one million, the largest city in the country to depend entirely on pumped ground water for survival. Phoenix receives only 7.8 inches of rain annually, and depends on its 1,265 miles of canals and on its complex of four dams on the Salt River and two on the Verde River to supply seventy-five percent of the water to sustain most of the city's 1.5 million people. The remainder of the needed water is pumped from the ground.

Water continues to be a crucial issue for the entire state. There is speculation that some day Tucsonans will be forbidden to do any landscape watering at all, but the city is devising ways to stop depleting its water table.

The Central Arizona Project (CAP) is a giant canal that brings Colorado River water to portions of Maricopa County (where Phoenix is located) and to Tucson. The CAP is still under construction and will cost more than 3.5 billion dollars. One of the CAP's political architects, U.S. Representative Morris K. Udall, reflecting the fears of many, has said: "If I could turn the clock back fifty years and do it all over again, instead of spending 3 billion dollars for a water plan that would let Tucson grow and turn Phoenix into another Los Angeles, I would have suggested we take land by the Colorado River, where we have the water, and build ten cities the size of Yuma [AZ, population 50,000]."

It is little wonder that in the last decade a few forward-thinking landscape architects and designers have tried to push yet another horticultural revolution, a return to the natural landscape of the desert. They are not suggesting a backyard of desolate-looking creosote bushes, but one planted with trees like mesquites, paloverdes, and ironwoods, which can be lush if nurtured with a little water. The native plants can also provide lovely blossoms as well as adequate shade.

In Phoenix, landscape architect Steve Martino, whose work appears in this section, has, over the years, determined to provide his clients with colorful, shaded environments, totally integrated into their desert sites. He advocates the use of native plants and perhaps the planting of a small expanse of water-intensive Bermuda grass as a place to rest the eye.

This may sound like common sense, but to an area that has been an oasis of irrigated farmland for a century, the idea is radical. "Desert landscaping" is a concept that has traditionally meant either a rough cacti garden or a lawn of glaring white decomposed granite, where the razor-sharp spines of a few barrel cacti menace children and pets.

For models, the born-again, desert-plant-loving architects like Martino have looked to Taliesin West, the Frank Lloyd Wright School of Architecture founded by the master in Scottsdale, Arizona, in the 1930s. Here the school rolls up a hill and the buildings and landscape are one—the perfect flowering of Wright's environmental approach to design. Martino also studied Italian architect Paolo Soleri's small studio, Cosanti, also in Scottsdale, where the elements of shade, trees, and the judicious use of water is playful, comfortable, and totally integrated into its desert site.

Martino and Tucson landscape architects like Rozena Harmony, Mary Rose Duffield, and Walter Rogers also credit Guy Greene, a Tucson landscape architect, with providing models with exquisitely designed landscapes and hardscapes (such as pools and concrete). Greene's negative-edged pools look like the essence of the idea of a pool—a cooling pond, far removed from the white concrete and blue tile of the tens of thousands of pools in Phoenix and Tucson.

Historically, Tucson has embraced the desert for personal landscapes with far more grace than Phoenix—but then the Santa Cruz Valley city was never designed to be an oasis, and its water supply has always been limited. But in both urban areas, more and more people are concerned about water consumption and high maintenance costs outside their front doors. Native plants are finding their places in the sun once again.

There are advantages in using native plants that go beyond cost and water usage. The natives attract pollinators and predators and automatically tap into the food chain, bringing even more life into the landscape.

Canal Grove

A Hidden Sanctuary in Suburban Phoenix

IN MANY PARTS of the urban Southwest, evidence of architectural history is as rare as summer rain. Yet some determined souls have sought to preserve what is left of Phoenix's architectural past.

Mary and Jim Wentworth not only love historic houses, but are of the rare breed who can withstand the challenge of a major restoration. After an eleven-year search, they found their 1915 sand-colored adobe house in 1985 in a suburban Phoenix setting.

The house is one of three or four remaining old adobes in an area filled with towering palm trees and circa 1950 ranch-style homes. Its hidden location, surrounded by giant eucalyptus trees sheltering an old-fashioned garden paradise, makes this one of the most unusual houses in central Arizona.

Until the latter part of the nineteenth century, much of the Phoenix area was a sparsely populated, mostly uninhabitable desert. The Arizona Canal, diverting water from the Salt River, changed the very nature of the terrain. Irrigated farmland began attracting new settlers, and Phoenix's growth began. But the flow of water into the canal was not stabilized—there were floods

On the eastern edge of this urban garden, a path edged with hardy and fragrant rosemary leads to these painted Adirondack chairs (LEFT).

A British racing-green delivery bicycle from Harrods in London spills over with cut flowers and foliage from the garden (ABOVE).

A string hammock, stretched in the shade between two giant eucalyptus trees, provides the perfect place for a late afternoon nap (ABOVE).

A collection of antique implements is used to make potpourri from dried garden flowers (LEFT).

Sunlight streams through the old fig tree in the center of the garden, from which hangs an antique birdcage bedecked with flowers and greenery (TOP RIGHT). Wild violets encircle the tree in early spring. A stone pathway winds through the back garden.

A stone rabbit the owner's found in England peeks through yellow snapdragons and other flowers of spring planted around a small birdbath in the southeastern corner of the garden (BOTTOM RIGHT).

followed by droughts—until the completion of the Roosevelt Dam northeast of Phoenix in 1911. In the years following, a wealthy Pittsburgh industrialist, Charles Gilliland, Sr., bought 100 acres of the irrigated farmland to establish a date ranch. Gilliland brought into the area thousands of exotic Arawan date palms and built a twenty-two-room Spanish Mission-style mansion for his family along with several adobe guest houses. One of these auxiliary structures grew to be the Mexican hacienda-style house with several outdoor "rooms" the Wentworths restored beside the Arizona Canal.

From the 1950s until 1974, the adobe guest house, located about a mile from the Gilliland main house, was owned by the honorary French consul of Phoenix, Paul Coze. He was a well-known local artist and teacher of art, and the hidden dwelling with its red-tiled roof will probably always live in the memory of the neighborhood as the "Coze House." The artist added a lovely high-ceilinged studio, which has been used as a living room by subsequent owners, including the Wentworths. The room's adobe fireplace was designed by the late Hispanic sculptor Jesus Corrall, whose family was among the earliest settlers of

The soft light of dusk settles on the bedroom wing of Casa Paloma (LEFT). The adobe parapet wall and inset logs are unusual and witty interpretations of materials used in Mexican hacienda-style houses. The current owners added the canvas awning in keeping with the spirit of the house.

In the center of the drive adjacent to the garden, the owners have placed a Mexican fountain (RIGHT).

Scottsdale. The Coze house was the site of many artists' "salons" as well as an annual Bastille Day celebration.

Coze died in the house, as did the next owner, astronaut John "Shorty" Powers. The Wentworths acquired the house from its fifth owner. By then, the house was in need of repair. The house sits on an oddly shaped lot wedged between two of the neighborhood's typical ranch-style houses. It is set back from the road, its existence marked on the street by two simple, low walls. The driveway appears to be an easement running through the neighbors' yards. When the Wentworths first drove up to the one-story flat-roofed house, they were greeted by tons of accumulated debris—including rusted appliances and pyramids of old wood. The current owners spent six months repairing the house, replacing the plumbing and electricity, replacing the original roof tiles, and clearing the grounds.

The house is unusual not only because of its longevity in an area where old houses have continually succumbed to the wrecker's ball, but also because of its gracious hacienda design. Instead of the more monolithic walls of Pueblo-style adobes, the house has stepped planes and a portal wrapping around the front. The roof of the portal is supported by vigas extending over the portal's flagstone floors.

The new owners added interest by reconstructing the entry, adding a rectangular window designed by Mary Wentworth. This was the only alteration the couple made to the exterior appearance of the house. On the interior, they updated the small but charming kitchen, and enclosed an area that became a laundry room. They also trimmed back foliage that had been growing for three-quarters of a century, if not more.

Mary Wentworth spent every day on the site during the restoration, often making on-the-spot decisions about the location of walls. But her real signature is the restored garden. A passionate gardener, she was determined to make the garden as unusual as the house. Her plan was first to clear an elliptical-shaped area in the middle of the drive for a grassy area bordered by a garden of cactus and annuals. Now this oasis in the center of the gravel drive has a rustic bench shaded by Aleppo pines, and is a preview of the delights to be found in the main garden.

At the back of the property, where the tall eucalyptus trees stand guard, the owner kept many unusual specimens already growing in the sun-shaded main garden—a beautifully shaped fig tree, a stand of bamboo, and jacarandas, blue-blossomed trees

with delicate leaves, among others. But after repairing an existing wooden platform deck, adding walkways of old brick, and creating borders adjacent to and within the back garden, Mary Wentworth planted what many Phoenix gardeners find almost impossible to grow in the area—a young weeping willow near the outbuilding (as yet unrestored, the owners use it for storage), early blooming wild violets beneath the fig tree, two apple trees (a golden apple and a Dorsett and Anna), two peach trees, lilacs, kumquats, and hundreds of antique roses, some of which were moved from the Wentworths' previous Phoenix home.

This is a spring garden, which is at its peak in the first week of April. This is when snapdragons, petunias, sweet peas, nasturtiums, and full, rich, many-hued bearded iris are in bloom. The iris bulbs the owner planted are specially bred for the low desert climate at a local iris farm. In March, blooming citrus trees—orange, grapefruit, and lemon—add to the wild violets to create the sweet aroma of paradise.

Hidden behind the house, just below the canal bank, is a spring vegetable garden where tomatoes ripen next to a kumquat tree. (Arizona has two vegetable growing seasons, fall and

A festooned straw gardening hat rests on a painted child's chair from Mexico (FAR TOP LEFT).

Potted geraniums provide spots of color around the house and garden (TOP LEFT).

A tile mosaic of Our Lady of Guadalupe is set into an exterior adobe wall beneath the portal (BOTTOM LEFT).

On an adobe wall in the outdoor dining room, a whimsical piece of Mexican pottery is embellished with garden cuttings (TOP RIGHT).

The entrance to *Casa Paloma*, the House of the Dove, is marked by this Mexican tile sign on a low adobe wall—the only visible sign on the street of the historic house in the midst of a 1950s-era subdivision (RIGHT).

Under the covered portal is the undulating wall of an outdoor banco adjacent to Casa Paloma's front entrance (LEFT). The name of its sculptor, Jesus Corrall, is signed in the adobe.

A potting shed with its charming awnings and painted door adds to the magical feeling of this hidden garden (RIGHT). The owner's designed the door; a friend completed the painting for her.

Sheltered on three sides by adobe walls of the house, this niche is a perfect outdoor dining area. The table setting reveals the ability to mix design elements: Mexican pottery and a traditional American quilt (BELOW).

spring.) Mary Wentworth is a gourmet cook and uses her tomatoes for a variety of Southwestern and French dishes. A small herb garden with a tiny sign urging people to *Please Touch* is tucked into an area by the front door of the house.

There are several outdoor rooms where the owners entertain guests, each with its own ambience. For informal breakfasts, the family sits at a heavy wooden picnic table on the wood deck that rims the back garden. For formal luncheons, they will serve at a table set in a niche in the exterior adobe walls of the house. This "room" is enclosed on three sides and is the coziest of the outdoor areas. Evening cocktails are often served on the porch outside the master suite, set with comfortably cushioned wrought iron furniture. Another table can be set for a dinner party for six on an uncovered bricked-in area near the portal that runs the length of the front of the house. Adobe *bancos* (benches) are built-in under the portal, and guests can sit on two wrought iron chairs grouped together for conversation.

The owners are active people and are parents of three grown boys. In 1985 the family gave a formal dinner party for the Christmas season for 350 people. They ingeniously utilized their

center drive for the catered, elegant event. Guests were safely and comfortably seated beneath an enormous white tent centered around the drive's Mexican fountain.

More recently, the garden served as the site for a niece's wedding for 200 guests in attendance. White chairs faced the formal garden, and the floral designers draped white tuille high above the wedding party in the giant eucalyptus trees.

Mary Wentworth is a self-proclaimed romantic and as often as not, guests for dinner in the garden will be treated to the playing of "Tea for Two" on an old portable crank phonograph. She collects blossoms to make her own potpourri, and has demonstrated the process to luncheon guests using antique utensils designed specifically for the sifting and straining necessary to create the dried bouquets.

The new owners of the former guest house have become impeccable stewards of the house and garden. To take a moment's rest on the hammock in the garden, in full view of rare lavender-hued roses, is an experience not easily duplicated anywhere else in the low desert of Arizona.

Furnished with casual *equipale* (pigskin) furniture from Mexico, the portal outside the master bedroom is a peaceful place for coffee and the morning paper (ABOVE).

A cement table with two painted iron garden chairs furnishes the wooden deck just outside the low garden wall (RIGHT).

Desert Drama

A Cactus Sculpture Garden in Carefree

Driving north from the metropolitan Phoenix and Scottsdale area, the housing developments and office complexes give way to stretches of unadulterated Sonoran Desert. Here, the terrain is hilly and higher than in the city, and the arid landscape lush with saguaros, palo verde, ironwood, and mesquite trees.

Less than a generation ago, the Desert Foothills, as this area is known, was sparsely populated with hardy cattle ranchers, solitary "desert rats"—miners and mineralogists in search of gold, onyx, and jasper—and so-called lungers, who found relief from respiratory ailments with the dry desert air. In the late 1950s, however, two developers, Tom Darlington and K. T. Palmer, saw money, if not gold, in those boulder-strewn hills, and the town of Carefree came into being. Through their development efforts, a small community blossomed amid the rocks and hills. Gracious houses were built, nestled into the desert setting, giving shelter to those who wished to escape the congestion of metropolitan Phoenix or the cold winters of other parts of the country.

It was the lure of the outdoors and the wish to avoid the cool, damp winters of their native northern California that brought Joyce and Gene McGillicuddy

An iron gate, which allows visitors a glimpse of the front courtyard, replaced a solid wooden door (LEFT). The ceramic wall hanging is a work by Christopher Heede, an Arizona artist. The pots are from Mexico, made of handcarved stone. The container on the right is planted with a small ocotillo, a shrub native to the Southwestern deserts, whose whiplike branches can reach up to twenty-five feet high.

The trunk and leaves of the foothills palo verde tree are a beautiful shade of yellow-green (ABOVE). The drought-tolerant tree, native to the deserts of Arizona, attracts many birds. The desert trees in this garden were watered with a drip irrigation system only for the first few months after they were planted.

A *Cereus peruvianus* and golden barrel cacti share a corner of the garden (FAR LEFT). Granite boulders add texture and interest throughout the landscape.

The curving shapes of the garden walls help to define the landscape and its pathways. The plastered walls, added during the landscape remodeling, were inspired by the Pueblo style of the house's architecture (MIDDLE LEFT).

The tall *Yucca rostrata* dominates a planter near the pool (LEFT). The multitrunked organ pipe cactus to the right is native to southern Arizona and parts of Mexico; it blooms at night. The silver-gray agave in the foreground completes the composition. The cobalt blue urn is by artist Christopher Heede, topped with a cholla "skeleton," the inner, woody structure of the cactus.

to Carefree. As sports enthusiasts, they wished to resettle in an area where they could be active outside year-round.

In 1983, the McGillicuddys found a house that met their needs. Set on two and a half acres at the base of Black Mountain, the house is built in a contemporary Pueblo style, with a flat roof, protruding vigas, and buff-colored plaster walls. A series of set-backs and differing roof heights provide contrast to the house's basic rectangular plan. For the McGillicuddys, the property's guest house, tennis court, and pool/spa combination were deciding factors in the purchase of the house, as were the lovely views of Phoenix to the south and Black Mountain to the north.

Built in the early 1980s, the house has a simple floor plan. A central living room is flanked on one side by a guest bedroom and a study, and by the master suite, kitchen, and dining alcove on the other. French doors link the living room, master suite, and study to the south-facing pool patio; the kitchen opens up onto a small, walled patio to the north. The McGillicuddys asked Carefree interior designer Isabel Ballerna to help them with a decor for the house that was distinctly Southwestern; sun-washed colors, rustic textures, and arts and crafts from local artists were chosen to complement the interior architecture.

Though the abode's interior required only furnishings to make it livable, the exterior needed a bit more polish. During the construction of the house, much of the surrounding acreage had been scraped clean by the previous owners, save for a few desert trees and saguaros. Weeds and the prolific shrub desert broom grew back where once low-spreading cactus and mesquite had grown. Closer to the house, around the angled pool and its flagstone patio, subtropical plantings such as queen palms, bougainvillea, and gazanias were struggling to thrive in Carefree's higher altitude. At approximately 2,200 feet in elevation, damaging frosts are a common occurrence in Carefree during the winter months; temperatures can easily dip as low as eighteen degrees Fahrenheit in January.

As pleased as the McGillicuddys were with the house and its recreational amenities, they wanted to remodel the landscape so that it both reflected their newly found interest in the desert as well as integrated the house more completely into the surrounding arid landscape. For help with the grounds, they turned to landscape designer Marcus Bollinger with the Scottsdale firm of Landscaping by André.

The landscape designer first tackled the property's serious physical problem before turning his attention to aesthetics. The site sloped from north to south. During the summer and winter rains, rivulets of water streamed down from the slopes of Black Mountain straight toward the house. Marcus Bollinger suggested regrading the lot, creating a series of undulating contours

that would not only match those of the surrounding natural desert, but divert water away from the house. Before any new planting took place, some 8,000 yards of dirt were moved on the site to create gentle hills and vales. On the northern—and highest—side of the property, a rock-lined swale was constructed to catch the first rush of rainwater.

Though there were some existing walls surrounding the immediate house and pool area, the landscape designer added more walls to define the perimeter of the property. The low, softly curving walls, plastered in the same shade as the house's exterior walls, link the house to the landscape and also serve to delineate the walkways through the garden, as well as the property's two driveways.

Prickly pear, cholla, and other cacti grow alongside the low, undulating garden wall that defines the perimeter of the property. The contemporary, Pueblo-style house is nestled into the sloping site, with views of the city to the south and mountains to the north. The garage and its driveway are on the right, separated from the formal driveway and entrance to the house, which are on the opposite side of the building (ABOVE LEFT).

Along the front drive, the polka-dot prickly pear cactus displays its showy blossoms in the early spring months (ABOVE). During the relandscaping of the property, decomposed granite was used as the ground cover material, as it closely matches that of the natural desert floor.

A cushioned *banco*, or built-in bench, is a cool spot for lounging on the portal. The portal, adjacent to the living room, is decorated as an extension of the indoors. The patio material is a salmon-hued flagstone; the twig chair is from Carefree Concepts, Carefree (LEFT).

The coral blossoms of the hesperaloe provide a subtle stroke of color against the monochromatic background (ABOVE). The flowers are particularly attractive to hummingbirds.

The golden barrel cactus receives an extra shower of color from the yellow palo verde blossoms. The cactus, a native of Mexico, can grow up to two and a half feet in diameter (ABOVE MIDDLE).

The blossoms of the palo verde tree shine in the early morning sunlight. The upright cardon cactus and agaves cast intriguing shadows on the garden wall (ABOVE RIGHT).

The front approach to the house, located on the east side, was given a new sense of drama. The original gravel driveway that leads to the entry courtyard was paved in a shadow gray, textured, stamped concrete material, giving the approach a sense of formality. The front driveway curves around an old palo verde tree, enshrined by a new, raised circular planter. In the spring, the drive is blanketed by the tree's chartreuse blossoms. The landscape designer replaced the old wooden door to the small entry courtyard with a wrought iron gate, allowing visitors a peek into the tiny garden and a view of the front door. The property's second driveway was also paved with the gray concrete material.

On the north, just off the kitchen, a small beehive-shaped barbecue was built into a corner of the garden wall. The tennis court also was fine-tuned to fit into the new landscape with the addition of shade ramadas built on either side of the court. The walls surrounding the court were also bermed with dirt, softening the effect of the high walls and, in turn, sinking the court below grade and out of sight.

Once the hardscape was in place, the plantings were given careful consideration. As newcomers to the desert, the McGillicuddys were intrigued by the subtle beauty of the native plants. However, the re-creation of a natural desert look was virtually impossible for their garden, as most of the indigenous plant material was removed when the house was built. Marcus Bollinger suggested another option—the creation of a desert garden based on a theme of collecting cactus as "sculpture." Specimens would be grouped together and displayed with the same care as works of art.

The fading palms and bougainvillea were removed, as was a small grove of olive trees in a narrow, walled garden next to the kitchen courtyard. In place of the original plants are cacti such as the spherical golden barrel, ribbed *Cereus peruvianus*, cholla, prickly pear, artichoke agave, and dagger-tipped yuccas, interspersed with carefully positioned granite boulders. In the small entry court, the landscape designer set the tone for the garden with a choice *Yucca rostrata*, the fuzz-covered "grandfather" cactus, and the unusual, rootlike boojum tree. The search for the cacti is a long-term commitment. If the owners find a particularly beguiling specimen, they make special room in the garden for it to flourish.

Although the McGillicuddys viewed the cactus as sculpture in the garden, they also worked in some "real" sculpture in the form of ceramic pieces. They commissioned Arizona artist Christopher Heede to create works for the garden walls near the entry, large urns for the pool patio, and opalescent ceramic tiles for the outdoor fireplace on the kitchen patio.

Away from the house, Texas sage, palo verde, and mesquite trees were planted to screen the house from the street. Although the hues in the landscape are basically shades of green, pink *Salvia greggi*, blue ruellia, and coral-blossomed hesperaloe add subtle touches of other colors during the spring months.

A citrus grove, sunken between the pool and the tennis court, is the only concession to non-native species. The designer grouped the deep-green-leafed trees together for impact, rather than spreading them out throughout the landscape. The orchard, kept low so that there would still be a view from the pool patio above, yields limes, tangelos, Valencia and Arizona sweet oranges, tangerines, and pink grapefruit. Though all of the new plantings—except for the citrus—are drought-tolerant native

A citrus orchard was planted below the pool patio so that the trees would not block views of the city to the south. The house also has views of Black Mountain to the north. The giant saguaro cactus on the right was preserved from the original landscape (ABOVE).

A narrow courtyard accessible from the kitchen is planted with a sculptural display of cacti and desert trees (RIGHT). The shapes of the tall, upright *Cereus peruvianus*, the spray of the swordlike desert spoon leaves, and the lacy shoestring acacia and blue palo verde trees play well off one another. In the background, the raised beehive fireplace and outdoor furniture create a comfortable kitchen patio.

122

species, an automatic watering system was installed to help the plants become established and grow more quickly than they would under natural rainfall conditions. The irrigation is turned on in measured quantities during the warmer months, and is virtually shut off during the cool winter season.

The owners furnished their outdoor spaces with an emphasis on comfort. Sleek, contemporary patio furniture from Tropitone is used poolside; a rustic table and twig chairs create an outdoor dining room on the portal overlooking the pool. Cushioned *bancos*, or benches, on the portal provide more seating. The kitchen patio is also simply furnished with contemporary outdoor chairs and tables.

The house and its updated landscape provide a wonderful backdrop for the couple's sports and entertaining needs. Both husband and wife play tennis and swim. Most days, he trains for bicycle racing on the hilly, curving roads of Carefree, while she prefers walking the roads and trails closer to the house. On weekends, the guest house is often filled with their children and grandchildren, who have come to enjoy the poolside barbecues, and mornings on the kitchen patio with coffee and newspapers.

There are new delights to discover daily. During the winter months, a flotilla of colorful hot air balloons, launched from a nearby resort, drift by silently in the valley below. A resident squirrel has taken to drinking from the pool fountains; an owl often perches on the tennis court wall, keeping score. Javelinas and coyotes roam through the yard behind the court, and the pool patio served as a rookery for ten baby quail. Finally, at the end of each day, the glowing lights of Phoenix look like tiny crystals set against black velvet, and the silence of the desert is restorative.

A gravel drive was made into a formal, circular driveway, anchored by the chartreuse-blossomed foothills palo verde tree (LEFT). The arched gateway leads to the small entry courtyard. The drive is paved in Bomacron, a stamped concrete material.

During the landscape remodeling, the property was regraded, and earth was bermed up along the tennis court walls, creating the look of a sunken court. The homeowners built the shade ramada and bench (TOP RIGHT).

The pool patio offers enough space for relaxation and entertaining. The steps lead up to the portal and the living room. A canvas market umbrella shades the Tropitone furniture. The patio material is flagstone (BOTTOM RIGHT).

n Setting

A Natural
esertscape
n Carefree

SINCE THE Second World War, the metropolitan Phoenix/Scottsdale area has enjoyed unprecedented growth. Its arid climate and surrounding desert have been magnets for those who seek escape from the harsh winters and industrialized cities of the East.

Central Phoenix, however, has long since ceased to be a "desert." Settled more than a century ago by pioneers who greened the land with irrigation and agriculture, the city's natural desert land could only be found farther and farther in the outskirts. As more housing has been built to accommodate the population, the fragile land has been scraped clean and replanted with greenery imported from other climates.

Since the 1970s, concern about the availability of water to sustain the population growth and a movement to preserve portions of the Sonoran Desert have surged to the fore. Throughout the region, architects and landscape designers have become more and more conscious of integrating new housing projects into the desert, taking advantage of the subtlety of the surrounding materials, colors, and contours. For use in gardens, many designers are now

Set on a ridge in the high desert above Carefree, the house is integrated into the saguaro-filled site through the use of natural colors, earth berms, and native landscaping. The homeowners have used the grounds surrounding the house to display an intriguing collection of sculpture (LEFT).

The lacy branches of the young palo verde tree in bloom are a festive contrast to the taupe-plastered exterior walls (ABOVE).

A south-facing ramada overlooks a stretch of desert (LEFT). The landscape architect revegetated portions of the five-acre property that were disturbed during the house's construction, as well as an old jeep road that cut through the lot. Ocotillo, prickly pear, cholla, brittlebush, and other desert natives were planted in a "random" manner emulating nature. The landscape architect walked the site with cans of colored spray paint; each colored dot of paint on the ground signified the location of a different plant.

Recessed windows and a stepped-back facade create interest in the architecture, as well as dramatic points in which to plant young palo verde trees and ocotillo (BELOW). Water from the *canale*, or drain spout, drips into the garden below.

choosing native species, which use little water and match the surrounding Sonoran landscape.

Such was the case with a house built in the lush desert hills of Carefree, some thirty miles north of downtown Phoenix. The homeowners, a couple whose primary residence is in the Pacific Northwest, are not newcomers to the desert environment. They previously owned a house in Palm Desert, California, as well as another house in Carefree. But when they began planning this particular house, they knew that they wanted it to be more connected with the desert than their former residences through careful siting, views, and preservation of the natural surrounding landscape.

Lovers of the outdoors, the couple found a five-acre parcel of land situated on a "shelf" of level land just above their favorite Carefree golf course. The lot was covered with low desert scrub, and dotted with saguaros and palo verde trees, and was bisected by an abandoned jeep road (forged by those who had worked a nearby ranch) and an arroyo, or dry wash. The couple was captivated by the views of Continental Mountain to the north and other mountains and distant city to the south.

At the front entry, a desert "vignette" gives visitors a hint of the rest of the landscape (LEFT). A columnar saguaro, the thin, leafy branches of the upright ocotillo, the rounded pads of the prickly pear, and the yellow-blossomed brittlebush are common sights on the Sonoran Desert of Arizona.

The landscape architect created earth berms along one side of the house to block views of a nearby roadway and to visually sink the house into the site. A by-product of the berming process was the elevation of the desert floor to windowsill height, allowing the homeowners a closeup view of desert life. From an indoor game table, one can see the feeding area and its stream of visitors, including quail, wrens, and ground squirrels (BELOW).

Before they began construction in the mid-1980s, the owners placed a few benches on various points of the property, so they could sit and contemplate the positioning of the future house.

The couple asked Carefree architect Terry Kilbane, whose work in the contemporary Southwest style they admired, to design the house. Scottsdale landscape architect Steve Martino was engaged to create outdoor living spaces that were in harmony with the elevated site. Martino is well known for his natural, arid-region designs and his strong advocacy of desert preservation. The two architects worked together from the blueprint phase of construction.

The three-bedroom, 3,500-square-foot house is set approximately in the middle of the acreage, its architecture evocative of a Pueblo Revival style—with a very contemporary twist. The taupe-plastered exterior walls are massive and protective, yet deeply recessed doorways and windows and a stepped-back roofline keep the house from overwhelming the site. The flat roof and *canales*, or drain spouts, are typical of the traditional Pueblo motif, but the house's lines are crisp, angled. The architect put the flat roof to good use. A steep set of exterior stairs on the

A dried century plant and
ocotillo branches in a pot
add texture and interest to a
side wall of the house.

Allan Houser's limestone
sculpture *Earth Mother* is
seemingly at home against a
backdrop of pink penstemon
and yellow palo verde
blossoms (RIGHT).

west side leads up to a sun deck—and magnificent views of the desert hills.

Entered from the north side, the interior of the house is anchored with an open kitchen and living and dining area. A niche for a game table is just off the dining area. The master suite and a study are to one side, and the guest bedrooms are at the opposite end of the house. An attached garage angles off from the northern side of the house.

The couple had the interior furnished in a spare, modern style to underscore their collection of antique and contemporary Native American pottery, and works by artists from the Northwest and Southwest. The architect gave the owners their most important works of art, "displayed" in each room of the house (including the shower in the master bath)—windows that neatly frame selected views of the desert.

Outdoors, the landscape architect faced his own set of challenges—creating an environment that enhanced the architecture, yet minimized the impact of the house on the land. One of the first hurdles overcome was the positioning of the driveway. A simple solution might have been to bulldoze a path from the garage to the road below, but that would have created a scar visible from miles away. Instead, Martino suggested excavating a curving driveway, thereby sinking it below grade and out of sight. To further lessen the drive's impact, it was paved in decomposed granite, a material that closely matches that of the natural desert floor.

The earth from the excavation of the driveway and that of the pool and septic tank was put to good use on the property. Although the landscape architect utilized the curves of the ridge-top site in his plan, he improved on nature a bit by building up the land on the eastern side of the house, closest to the road. The earth berms come right up to the house, lifting the level of the desert floor to windowsill height. This gives the homeowners an immediate view of the desert's flora and fauna, even while seated, and blocks their view of the road below. Viewed from far away, the berms shorten the height of the house, and serve to sink it into the site. More earth berms were used to camouflage service areas around the house.

While the homeowners were concerned with blending the house into the environment, they also wished to enjoy outdoor amenities, such as patios and a pool. Martino created a series of multilevel patios on the southern and western sides of the house,

Near the front entry, Allan Houser's Native American figure treads lightly on a granite boulder (TOP LEFT). The piece, visible from the drive, sets the tone for the rest of the garden. The window behind it allows the owners to view the artwork from within the house, too.

Set in a bed of lavender-hued verbena, the prickly pear is a natural desert sculpture. New growth are the "ears" sprouting at the top of the old pads. The prickly pear's fruit is edible and often made into jams and candy (BOTTOM LEFT).

A deeply recessed front doorway, flat roof, and protruding canales signal a Pueblo Revival style of architecture. However, the crisp lines of the house, intriguing angles, and stepped-back facade indicate a thoroughly contemporary interpretation. A meandering pathway of flagstone from Ash Fork, Arizona, and garden walls create an interesting approach (TOP RIGHT).

A low, angled garden wall (RIGHT) draws visitors to the front door on the right and points to the garage approach on the left. The multibranched saguaro is slow-growing and old. The cactus, columnar when young, rarely sprouts "arms" before the age of seventy-five. It blooms in late spring, and the saguaro fruit is edible. The figure is by Allan Houser.

as well as a private patio just off the master suite. Paved in a pale salmon flagstone, the patios are set lower than the house, so that outdoor furniture does not block views from indoors.

To further preserve views from indoors, Martino positioned the forty-eight-foot-long lap pool and a spa on the western side of the house, where windows are minimal. The pool is cantilevered over the arroyo; at the westernmost edge of the pool patio, there is a steep drop-off to the desert below. For that reason, the ordinance-mandated safety fence that prevents people from entering the pool area was not necessary on that side, allowing swimmers an uninterrupted view of the desert beyond. An outdoor fireplace, used in the fall and winter months, takes the chill off an evening swim. To encourage the owners to experience more of their desert land, a set of stairs from the pool patio leads down to the arroyo, and a barely visible trail winds around the property.

The homeowners added a shade ramada over the patio adjacent to the living and dining area. Furnished simply with contemporary outdoor furniture, the protected patio has become their al fresco dining room. More furniture of the same type provides comfortable seating around the pool and on the bedroom patio.

In selecting plantings, the landscape architect used not only a sense of design, but a sensitivity to the patterns of nature. Much of the landscaping was actually a restoration of the natural desert. Close to the house, in the patio areas, raised planters are filled with desert "vignettes," plants selected for their texture, color, and mass, and to give a hint of what is likely to be found in the surrounding land. Tall, whiplike ocotillo, yellow-blossomed brittlebush, penstemons, *Salvia greggi,* shrimp plants, and prickly pear cacti make appearances in beds around the house. The more domesticated ground covers, lantana and verbena, were added for color near the house.

Although the building "envelope" was carefully respected during the course of construction, areas around the house had to be revegetated after building was completed. Major trees and cacti moved during construction were replanted. Their survival was ensured through careful positioning; tender sides once again faced north, and sunburned, calloused sides again faced southwest. Ironwood trees, which usually grow at a lower elevation than the property's 2,800 feet, were brought in to provide more height to the plantings. Martino planned the revegetation of the

The bubbling, hot waters of the spa are soothing and therapeutic. The wall provides a bit of privacy; the beds are filled with reminders of the desert beyond (ABOVE LEFT).

An outdoor fireplace and a thick towel take the chill off an early evening swim during the cooler winter months (ABOVE).

A forty-eight-foot lap pool, framed by prickly pear and ocotillo, provides ample room for exercise. The stained wood sculpture at the end of the pool is by Oregon artist Eugene Bennett. Beyond the far wall, a row of solar collectors heat the pool and provide hot water for the house (LEFT).

The subtle landscape is the perfect foil for a collection of contemporary art displayed in areas around the house. Just off the ramada, this bronze—a stylized vision of a Native American water-bearer—is by Santa Fe, New Mexico, sculptor Allan Houser (LEFT).

The lap pool and spa (RIGHT) are located on the west side of the house, to preserve desert views to the south from the living and dining area. The patio material is flagstone, its buff tone blending with the color of the desert floor. The steps on the left lead to a sun deck. The metal gate separates the pool area from the ramada, which is open to the desert beyond. The mesh at the bottom of the gate prevents rabbits from nibbling at young growth in the planters surrounding the pool.

old four-wheel-drive road by first walking the road with cans of spray paint, indicating with different sprayed dots of color where the shrubs and cacti should "randomly" be replanted.

A drip irrigation system was installed to give the new plantings—both in the beds near the house and in the revegetated zones—a chance to become established. The landscape architect estimates that for two years it is necessary to provide small amounts of water for the replanted and newly planted desert natives; after that, they are on their own. Except for occasional pruning of trees and shrubs near windows and doorways, the garden is virtually maintenance-free.

The homeowners have added their unique touch to this natural setting. As much as their interior is visually enriched with art, they wanted the outdoors to be similarly enhanced. The couple collect major pieces of sculpture by New Mexico artist Allan Houser, and nestle his stylized visions of Native American women among desert plants and on patios. Exterior wall hangings and works by other artists also provide a sense of serendipity when viewing the landscape for the first time.

When they are in residence during the winter and spring months, the couple finds their desert house rewarding and calming. They are often visited by grown children and grandchildren. The pool and sun deck are put to good use (the sun deck being a favorite with grandchildren who like to sleep under the stars), and barbecues are frequent.

When the owners are alone, the subtle pleasures of the desert are more evident. Just outside the window by the game table, they have set up a feeding area for desert denizens: quail, cardinals, and ground squirrels munch on the seeds. Deer and javelinas, attracted by a salt lick, stomp through the feeding patch; the owners were once startled to see a javelina's snout pressed up against the window when they glanced up from a card game.

During the day, there are hikes to be taken into the surrounding hills and canyons, and golf games to be won on the course below. But, perhaps, evenings are best. With a knitting project in her hands and a book in his, they sit on the patio and feel the breezes come down the mountain and the sun's warmth fade behind the distant hills.

Creekside Splendor

A Traditional Tucson Ranch in the Heart of Bear Canyon

T HE SANTA Catalina Mountains are part of an ancient land, where twelve million years ago volcanic forces began to push up the earth to form the most visible mountains in Tucson. Humans first came here 12,000 to 15,000 years ago, predating by thousands of years the well-known Hohokam people.

Today, part of the canyons and creeks of the Catalinas are protected by the sheltering arms of the Coronado National Forest. This is on the extreme eastern border of the Sonoran Desert, and until the early twentieth century, one of the Catalina's canyons, Sabino Canyon, was an access route to the high country—Mount Lemmon at about 9,000 feet and Mount Bigelow, 8,500 feet. In this century, Sabino Canyon has been gently developed into an internationally known recreation area.

Hikers and walkers explore the upper and lower canyons especially when Sabino Creek runs, nine to eleven months of the year. A favorite time of hikers is mid to late summer, when the creek is at its most swollen—the result of intense late summer squalls. One of the most beautiful hikes within the Sabino Canyon area is to Seven Falls, which is over a high saddleback ridge

Tucson's mountains majesty—the Santa Catalinas—mark the landscape for miles. Their canyons and creeks have given shelter, sustenance, and beauty to man for thousands of years (LEFT).

The smooth rocks of the creekbed shine in the morning light of spring, when the water of the creek diminishes to intermittent small pools (ABOVE).

into Bear Canyon. Here, Bear Creek plunges 500 feet down a series of shelves and forms seven waterfalls, interspersed by refreshing, cool pools.

It was near Seven Falls along Bear Creek that John and Elaine Stilb, along with their seven children, began an adventure in ranch and desert living that has continued for a generation.

The origin of their Bear Canyon Ranch, which is surrounded on two sides by national forest land, seems to be in the late nineteenth century, when only the brave attempted life in the desert. The Stilbs believe their low, native stone ranch house, now set on twenty-six acres, was built about the turn of the century; the house appears on county maps as early as 1904.

A chance meeting by one of the Stilb daughters and a former resident of the ranch produced some rare and remarkable photographs. A 1929 snapshot shows a two-story house with a wide, peaked roof and a second-story veranda. Another, taken about the same time, reveals scrub desert almost to the riparian plain of the creek. When the Stilbs bought the house in the 1950s, the second story had been lost to fire and much of the scrub desert surrounding the house had given way to a variety of landscapes.

It turns out the Stilbs were almost as brave as Bear Canyon Ranch's earliest settlers. The rectangular, flat-roofed house had endured innumerable remodelings in a half-century and had been seriously neglected for a number of years. The house had dark green cement floors and stuffed animal heads in every corner, the legacy of its previous owner, a big game hunter.

The Stilbs embarked on their first, major, remodel in 1955 after a fire (the house has more or less survived at least three major conflagrations in its history) and then another refurbishing five years later. They completely restructured and modernized the kitchen, enclosed a porch with wide windows to create a family room and dining area with a full view of the west side of the ranch, installed Saltillo tile flooring, and added two long portals on either side of the house.

Ranch life continued to require pluck and imagination. Snakes were everywhere, and Elaine Stilb had to learn to shoot a gun to protect her young children on the property. While they were remodeling, a makeshift kitchen had to be moved to the front porch where birds often feasted on family meals. During the 1950s and sixties, the ranch was still so far from the services of Tucson that simply driving seven children to various schools each morning was a major undertaking. For two decades the family

The free-form, negative-edged pool with a discreet waterfall was designed to echo the water of Bear Creek, which, like the pool, is an integrate part of life at the ranch.

Early morning light slants across the traditional stone ranch house of Bear Canyon Ranch. The house was built around the turn of the century, and cattle grazed here on open range up until the 1950s. In the 1960s, the Stilbs added portals on the east and west sides of the house (MIDDLE LEFT).

The Santa Catalinas and the setting sun provide the breathtaking setting for an evening dinner on the brick-paved rise near the pool (BOTTOM LEFT).

A Mexican fountain is the dramatic focal point of the main entryway to the east portal and the lawn beyond (RIGHT).

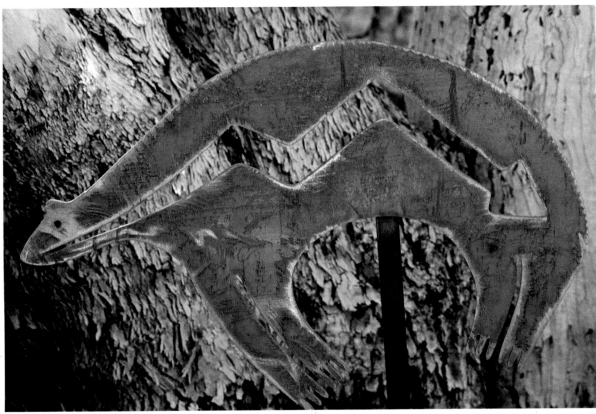

The stone guest house of Bear Canyon Ranch. The blue front door, with its glossy white-trimmed side lights and lintel, are flourishes of the Territorial architectural style (LEFT).

This bear (ABOVE), the symbol of Bear Canyon, is a Zuni fetish with power second only to the mountain lion. He is the ruler of the west. He brings good hunting, safe travel, and good luck.

managed with a slow unreliable well and often had to siphon water from springs on a nearby hill. In summer, when the well ran dry, they had to take their laundry into town to use washing machines with free-flowing water, and John Stilb jokes that he joined a local country club just so his four daughters would have somewhere to wash their hair. In 1976, they successfully drilled a new well. It took drilling equipment used in mines to bore down 237 feet to reach water.

The Stilbs feel they have lived in the out-of-doors for almost four decades, and they have added significant landscaping and sheltered, shaded outdoor rooms to the ranch.

The west portal overlooking Bear Creek has become the major extension of the house to the outside and is the heart of outdoor family living. Here, Elaine Stilb has created a series of sitting areas with chairs, sofas, and small tables where meals are sometimes served and family members sit long into the evening.

The portals are set with pots of substantial, mature plants spilling over their sides—geraniums, jade plants, ivy, even small Aleppo pines—adding cooling greenery to the shaded porches. In spring, Elaine Stilb, who loves to garden, plants scores of pots with annuals—petunias, pansies, and snapdragons.

Some years ago the family added a patio between the guest house and the main house, now delightfully overrun with tiny flowering vincas. They also nurtured an expanse of lawn beyond the east portal, which has been the scene of countless touch football and croquet games.

Around the ranch the Stilbs have added to and cared for eucalyptus, acacia, mesquite, and palo verde trees planted by previous owners amid prickly pear and other cacti. These are the trees that have dramatically altered the landscape of the ranch from its earliest days.

Long before the Stilbs bought the property, cattle once had the run of the place and previous owners kept a gaggle of geese. When his children were young, John Stilb, once a passionate polo player, kept a dozen horses at the ranch, and children on horseback had the run of the place. Rabbits, squirrels, and even porcupines, which munch on the sycamore bark, have always been a part of the ranch. Over the years the family has seen javelinas, badgers, and even mountain lions, bobcats, and Mexican wolves near their property and within Bear Canyon. White-tailed deer love the ridge between Bear and Sabino canyons.

This breezeway connects
the vinca-entwined patio
between the guest and
main houses with an
expanse of lawn beyond
the east portal. The blue-
trimmed door is a side
entrance to the guest house
(FAR TOP LEFT).

On the west portal, a
simple bench is framed by
a white-trimmed window
set into a stone wall. The
portals are set with pots of
mature palms, geraniums,
ivy, even small Aleppo
pines (TOP LEFT).

The west portal faces Bear
Creek and is the major
extension of the house to
the out-of-doors. Furnished
with bright canvas-covered
cushions set upon simple
wood outdoor furniture,
the family spends many
intimate evenings here
(BOTTOM LEFT).

From the natural boulders
is a view of the east portal
and the family room
chimney (RIGHT).

Bear Creek is an integral part of life at the ranch. During a dry season, a previous owner built a small dam, a mosaic of smooth rocks from the stream set in concrete, which ensures a swimming hole even when the creek is low. Tall grasses reach out of the creek and large rocks worn smooth by coursing water show themselves during times of low water. Willows, cottonwoods, and local Sabino trees, similar to cypresses, are lush along the water, the traditional center of play for the Stilb children. During high water they would ride the rapids in inner tubes, walk back and ride them again, or run the rocky terrain straight uphill to Seven Falls. Otherwise, the children would organize major "wars" along the creek as well as treacherous "Amazon" cruises.

Five years ago the Stilbs built a dark, negative-edged, free-form pool set with boulders and a discreet waterfall and whirlpool, which shines like a jewel between the creek and the house. The planting beds around the pool are framed with railroad ties and are filled with annuals in spring in the midst of a hardy ground cover with tiny white flowers.

A brick patio around the pool is set with a white metal glass-topped table, and in spring and summer the table is often sheltered by a wide canvas umbrella. John and Elaine Stilb often sit here alone during Tucson's pink, white, and fuscia sunsets, watching the shift of colors on the Catalina Mountains. Blue herons fly overhead, and a red cardinal bathes several times each evening in a corner of the pool. After dark, small bats drink from the pool.

The gentle light of early morning streams across the brick-paved walkway around the pool. The owner was assisted by landscaper Phil Van Wyck in setting railroad ties and planting flower and shrub beds around the pool (ABOVE LEFT).

The clear light of late afternoon bathes the pool and trees (ABOVE). Olives, oleanders, seed Valencia oranges, and lemons surrounding the ranch survived years of neglect before the Stilbs bought the property. Some citrus trees popped up where the family happened to be watering something else. They were also surprised by a queen's wreath; the deciduous vine with heart-shaped leaves showed itself one day after a good rain.

An *equipale* (pigskin) table is set for a quiet dinner in the jewel-like tones favored by the owner. The dining area is one corner of a long family room with wide, sweeping windows allowing for views of the property as well as Bear Canyon (RIGHT).

Inside the house, the family room offers a sweeping view of the sunset. The room was planned with the simple elements of Southwestern design: Saltillo tile, built-in seating, and a curved fireplace (LEFT).

Saguaros on the eastern border of the Sonoran Desert reach up into the gold and mauve southern Arizona sunset (RIGHT).

The Stilbs have entertained hundreds of people outdoors at their ranch, and tiny Italian lights are permanent fixtures in the trees near the pool. When they serve dinner to a large group of people, as they have in recent years at the weddings of their children, Elaine Stilb hires the services of a local Tucson man, well known in his trade. The cook arrives at the ranch the evening before the event. He starts a fire of mesquite branches in an old underground kiln, once used by one of the Stilb daughters to fire clay pots. The cook tends the fire until four A.M., when he gently lowers a side of beef into the red-hot pit. He cooks it for eight hours, and also makes his own sauce from chilies and fresh oregano. The sauce is made in enamel pots and they, too, are buried in the mesquite fire.

The children and their friends all participated in the upkeep of the ranch. The Stilb children spent Saturdays and Sundays not only playing in the creek but awash with chores, too. Two sons built stone columns at the main entrance to the ranch; another built the patio near the guest house. At one side of the pool, a metal dragonfly sculpture was made by a daughter's friend.

These traditions continue. The Stilbs' adult children return often for weekends and holidays, bringing spouses to help with the chores and grandchildren to discover the wonders of the knocking of woodpeckers and the call of screech owls.

Spanish Masterpiece

A Joesler Adobe Still Reigns in Tucson's Catalina Foothills

OFTEN, THE INTERPLAY of light and clouds and mountains in the foothills of the Catalinas in Tucson makes for the most beautiful skies in all of southern Arizona. Perched on a promontory in these foothills overlooking horizon, desert, and rock is a remarkable peachy-pink mud adobe house, the crown jewel in a string of remarkable houses built in the 1940s in what was one of Tucson's first subdivisions.

The original owners of the Spanish-tiled-roof house, the Bauders, moved in on Pearl Harbor Day in 1941. Their architect was Josias Thomas Joesler, a native Swiss who studied his craft in Zurich, but lived in Morocco, Havana, Mexico City, and Los Angeles before moving to Tucson. It was Joesler who gave Tucson its first "look". He had soaked up enough knowledge of arid-region architecture to understand regional styles and desert-compatible living. The architect's career blossomed in Tucson, where he designed hundreds of houses from the very simple to those for wealthy winter visitors. After being eclipsed by more "modern" designs in the 1960s and seventies, "Joeslers" are now highly prized and much sought after in the city not only for their historical

A bottlebrush tree sits on an expanse of cooling lawn at the back of the house, with part of the portal in view (LEFT). The present owners have kept much of the house's original landscape.

The delicate dwarf poinciana is abloom here in the spring in the midst of spiny cactus (ABOVE).

A cool rattan daybed at one end of the screened outdoor dining room is a quiet, private place to read on warm afternoons. Above the wide daybed are painted floral windows in blue, white, and ocher, which are signed "1945 Ceionne."

A blazing fire in the outdoor living room takes the chill off the desert night after a late swim (RIGHT).

A shallow lap pool, fitted with exercise bars, was one of the few changes made by the new owners. The charcoal-plastered pool was designed by the owner with architect David Tyson (ABOVE).

The basic but elegant poolside furniture is reflected in the pool (LEFT). Beyond the privet hedge is a small courtyard surrounding an old olive tree.

In a back courtyard garden, an old olive tree is a haven for a statuette of Saint Francis and a place for contemplation (TOP and BOTTOM RIGHT).

interest but also for their unique beauty, design, and adaptability to the desert.

Although Joesler designed in many styles from Territorial and Pueblo to Art Deco, the Bauder house is in the Mexican Colonial style. Happily for its current owners, Patricia and Charles Blomfield, members of the Bauder family lived in the house for more than forty years. When the Blomfields bought the house in 1982 they bought an intact Joesler masterpiece, which had luckily escaped the modernizations and remodelings that have made other Joeslers virtually unrecognizable.

The current owners have lived in Texas, Alaska, and other places, and in 1982 they were on their way to build a house in Hawaii when they stopped in Tucson to visit friends. They never made it to the islands. As is true for countless visitors before them, they were captivated by the Old Pueblo, as Tucson is called. The Joesler home, buffered by twelve acres from neighbors and traffic, was the first house they saw. Patricia Blomfield fell in love with the four-decade-old dwelling at first sight.

The house, with its articulated facade, punctuated by deep windows protected by finely wrought grille work, eventually

Briefly aglow with late afternoon light, the romantic outdoor dining room is serene and cool. The room is furnished simply with oak trestle tables and a large china cabinet. Boston ferns on a ledge along the screened side of the porch add a lushness to the sheltered space (LEFT).

Adjacent to the screened dining room, the outdoor living room is protected under the deep overhang of the back portal. Family and guests sit here after dinner to enjoy the evening (TOP RIGHT).

A concrete lion at the front of the Mexican Colonial-style house is given fire and life in the dawn (BOTTOM RIGHT).

proved irresistible to Charles Blomfield as well. The new owners wanted to preserve the integrity of the house inside and out as much as possible. From its scored concrete-tile floors to its fine dark-wood beamed ceilings, the house was in good condition. The new owners were even able to leave the original cordovan paint on the ceiling of the library. The house had hidden treasures, too—a fourteenth-century door, which the owners understand was in a cache of treasures brought to the United States by William Randolph Hearst for his mansion, San Simeon.

As is the case with many older houses, the kitchen was inadequate. The new owners remodeled it immediately, adding sleek new cabinets and transforming a butler's pantry into a wine room. The rest of the house was left almost intact.

The architectural and environmental outdoor spaces of this house are captivating. Near the front entrance of the house, the owners have left the mature cactus garden with spectacular ocotillo, prickly pear, and all manner of agaves just as they found it, although they added low walls and brickwork. Just beyond the front door is a small, charming patio that serves a bedroom. The back of the house is composed of two outdoor rooms—a

screened-in dining room and a sheltered outdoor living room with a curved adobe fireplace. These seem to reflect the importance Joesler placed on outdoor living in the desert. The rooms overlook the backyard, which is enclosed by a low wall allowing for views of mountains on one side and city lights on the other. The new owners left the basic plan of the backyard garden intact, but added a shallow pool in the center of the yard.

The owners were quite fond of the original garden, and vowed to keep what they call its "old-fashioned" look. They kept the existing garden wall and neat privet hedge, and a cement seat around an ancient olive tree. Below the hedge are hundreds of geraniums that have happily survived two winters. Patricia Blomfield does much of the planting of flowers.

The house itself, although sited on a considerable rise, was not designed with enormous windows to take advantage of the views of the Catalinas or to let in the heat of the desert. For the enjoyment of the outdoors, Joesler wanted to bring people to two small terraces or into the covered exterior rooms. These outdoor rooms were the architect's signature, and they are ideal places for outdoor living throughout the year.

The screened-in dining room is designed to receive almost no direct sun. The beamed, tongue-and-groove ceilinged porch is a serene and cool oasis in warm months. The new owners added French doors leading from the kitchen, and surrounded them with shelves for philodendra. Other shelves, original to the house, run the full length on the screened side of the room and hold dozens of small potted Boston ferns, which add to the room's feeling of leafy comfort. A small cupboard near the French doors has a fold-out table. It was originally used for flower arranging and is now a liquor cabinet.

Patricia Blomfield has furnished this room simply, with two oak trestle tables seating twelve (practical for a couple with fourteen children and twenty grandchildren between them), a large china cabinet, and a rattan daybed tucked away to one side. The daybed is in constant use as a quiet place to read in the afternoons or as a bed for visitors who cannot resist the lure of a night spent on the porch. Next to the sleigh-style daybed is a small room once used by the original owners' butler, Foster, for hanging the keys of the realm and where the new owners found a tidy bundle of circa 1945 gardening magazines.

On a hill overlooking the Santa Catalina Mountains the adobe masterpiece by architect Josias Joesler still reigns on its original pristine desert site (LEFT).

Beyond the pool, bougainvillea blooms over the back of the garage and restored guest suite, which was once the butler's quarters. A sweeping bottlebrush tree obscures an entrance to the screened outdoor dining room (RIGHT).

Rejas (iron grilles) covering windows and sculptural onion domes above them are traditional architectural elements of the Mexican Colonial Revival style (FAR RIGHT).

For coffee and a view of the rising sun, the lure of this small terrace outside an east-facing guest bedroom is irresistible (BOTTOM RIGHT).

Every meal is eaten on the porch by the couple from early spring until November. Through a screened door, the owners—by themselves or with guests—enter into the outdoor living room in the evening with wine or coffee. Often after a late swim, the owners sit by the outdoor fireplace to warm themselves. The open room, its overhang supported by four vertical square dark-wood posts, is furnished with an equipale table, matching chairs, a low, carved bench, and a glass-topped table made from an old Mexican door.

The outdoor rooms are framed by enormous bottlebrush trees, red-plumed when in bloom in spring. Beyond the trees, the new pool, fitted with exercise bars, reflects light beautifully. Designed by Charles Blomfield in conjunction with Tucson architect David Tyson, the charcoal color of the mostly rectangular lap pool is integral with the plaster.

At the north end of the pool, bougainvillea grows over a room attached to the garage. Once the butler's quarters, the room was spruced up to provide space for houseguests, which sometimes number up to fifteen. Besides an almost constant flow of houseguests, the Blomfields entertain often. The outdoor dining room

(it was so designated by Joesler on the original plans for the house) can easily seat forty.

Dozens of terra-cotta pots are found at the front of the house on walkways and on the small terrace outside the library, around the pool, and at the entries to the outdoor rooms. They spill over with geraniums, succulents, rosemary, and agaves, and help create the well-tended but relaxed look found in the various places of the house.

Patricia Blomfield learned by trial and error what to plant in this particular desert area. In the late fall of their first year in the house, she planted 300 petunias. In a few hours, all the blossoms were gone, and by nightfall the plants were eaten down to the nubs—fine dining for desert rabbits inhabiting the neighborhood. Seeds for winter rye grass provided a feast for the birds. The owners love animals, but decided to plant flowers, such as geraniums, less beloved by rabbits and squirrels.

It is heartening to the Blomfields that this special house designed by Joesler has settled so well into its environment that they can still experience the desert as it once was in much of Tucson. Rabbits, squirrels, and owls are frequent visitors, and elsewhere on the property, coyotes, Gila monsters, and an occasional javelina have been seen.

Saguaro Castle

Contemporary Ranch House Simplicity in the Sonoran Desert

THE CANYONS of the desert near the Catalina Mountains in northeast Tucson make it one of the most varied and interesting desert habitats in the Southwest. On the southern face of the Catalina Mountains, at the head of Agua Caliente Creek, hot springs have soothed the aching muscles of hardy hikers for generations. The creek flows into the Agua Caliente Canyon, creating a riparian plain with a stretch of bright green in the otherwise pale palette of the desert.

The creek drops some 5,000 feet to the desert floor, where the cactus and rock of the desert and the richer plain near the creek come together in one of the most unusual spots in the Sonoran Desert. This is where Rick and Cindy Barrett chose to build their desert house, surrounded on three sides by mountains and in the midst of towering saguaro cacti.

Rick Barrett grew up in Tucson. He first explored the desert of northeast Tucson as a teenager with a new driver's license in the mid-1960s. His mother is a desert gardener, and he has always had a special feeling for the ecology of this delicate environment. This feeling is shared by Cindy Barrett, who grew up in a small desert community forty miles from Tucson.

The smoky, ethereal light of sunrise spills from the Santa Catalina Mountains onto the Sonoran Desert (LEFT).

The sheltering form of the blue-gray corrugated metal roof of the house rests delicately amid saguaro cacti, which can grow up to fifty feet and live for two centuries (ABOVE).

The house, a contemporary interpretation of the Arizona Territorial style, is built entirely of wood, rock, and concrete. Here, shadows fall over the ribbed fir front door (LEFT).

Covered porches wrap around the house. Outside the master suite, dappled light falls on willow chairs upholstered comfortably with pillows in the colors of the desert sky (TOP RIGHT). The chairs and pillows are from Home Decorator Fabrics in Tucson.

Outside on the terrace of the second-story loft, a small equipale table is set with the essentials for after-work Southwestern cocktails (BOTTOM RIGHT).

Early in their marriage, the Barretts lived in Tucson in a 1922 house they restored near the University of Arizona. In 1986, wary of what they considered inappropriate development of virgin desert around Tucson, the couple decided to build their dream house "while there was still desert to build in."

A year later they purchased the pristine desert lot perfect for them. Their four-acre site encompasses a section of the Agua Caliente Creek, and is thick with the tall and stately saguaros for which Arizona is famous. (The site is less than two miles from Saguaro National Monument, hundreds of acres of preserved desert with stands of the ancient cacti.) They knew they would build their future home in full view of the sights and sounds of the creek.

The Barretts chose Tucson architect Frank Mascia to work with them. On many Sundays for about a year, the architect would meet the couple on their lush high desert lot overlooking the creek to talk over ideas for the house. They knew the structure would be built on the lot's existing 16,000-square-foot clearing, which probably had been a holding pen for cattle at one time (the area was once part of a large ranch). Most of their four

The fluted ribs of a saguaro echo the pattern of the pitched roof.

The negative-edged dark pool, surrounded with natural boulders, seems to spill down the hill into the creekbed below (LEFT).

acres would be untouched, as their property extends well beyond the creek itself.

Originally, the couple thought they wanted a Santa Fe-style house with rough-hewn wood and massive walls. Yet what developed through these meetings (with the architect's gentle prodding) was a very contemporary home with fresh, witty reinterpretations in rustic materials—concrete, rock, and wood—of the traditions of early twentieth-century ranch houses in Arizona.

The orientation of the house was tricky—a balancing act between the ideal location for protection against the sun and the conservation of vegetation on the site. The form of the house followed the natural boundaries of important mesquite trees and saguaros as well as the shape of the clearing.

The architect tackled the organization of the interior spaces first, then worked out the exterior design. During their Sunday talks, the Barretts knew they wanted early morning sun in the living room and master bedroom and protection from the searing

afternoon rays. The architect laid out the house a half dozen times until he finally surveyed the site himself and found just the right angles.

What evolved was a low-slung house constructed with mauvish-brown split-faced block. The color of the block was carefully matched to the lot's soil to integrate the house into its setting. The design is dominated by a corrugated metal hipped roof of a blue-gray color that reflects the surrounding mountains. The roof determines the shape of the house—it is a sheltering form, a lid over the 2,600-square-foot home. Ribbed interior and exterior fir doors echo the pleating of the roof—all of which mimics the ridges of the saguaros on the site. Smooth river rocks were used for the house's fireplace, and scored concrete floors along with the metal roof are natural references to ranch house traditions.

A small second story houses a loft/den—humorously referred to by the architect and Rick Barrett as "the boy's room" or "the doghouse." On the peaked east side of this room, the architect

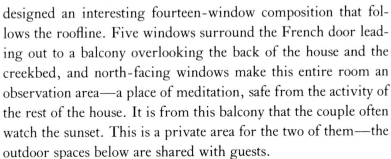

designed an interesting fourteen-window composition that follows the roofline. Five windows surround the French door leading out to a balcony overlooking the back of the house and the creekbed, and north-facing windows make this entire room an observation area—a place of meditation, safe from the activity of the rest of the house. It is from this balcony that the couple often watch the sunset. This is a private area for the two of them—the outdoor spaces below are shared with guests.

The back of the house faces not only the creek but a hill beyond and land of the Coronado National Forest. It is in the back outdoor spaces where the collaboration between architect and owners is most evident. The Barretts wanted outdoor "rooms" so comfortable and natural that they and their guests could feel a part of the desert. In addition, Rick Barrett wanted wide porches—he loves to walk them late at night and look at the desert.

While the roof is constant, the porches move in and out with the house's exterior walls and create outdoor rooms for sitting, walking, and eating. The porches, which also have concrete

A path of decomposed granite leads to the front door of the house; it is scarcely visible in the desert (FAR LEFT).

Paperflowers rustle in the wind (FAR MIDDLE LEFT). Native to Arizona and other Southwestern states, the drought-tolerant flowering plants are self-seeding and bloom from April until October.

On the creek overlook, an airy table set in white and blue for a summer dinner provides a shock of color against the tones of the desert (ABOVE LEFT).

The robust pink flowers of a hybrid *Echinopsis*, also known as a sea urchin cactus (ABOVE).

floors, cover 1,400 square feet. They are built at the same level as the house, and serve as extensions into the fragile desert itself.

A negative-edged, charcoal-colored pool with a natural boulder waterfall was planned for the last bit of open space on the lot once the house was designed. The pool was a compromise—Cindy Barrett wanted a lap pool and her husband wanted a "puddle." What resulted is what the couple call "the Barretts' desert watering hole." The boulders surrounding the pool are from the Agua Caliente Creek.

Two small planting areas near the pool are all the Barretts were willing to cultivate, other than adding more indigenous trees to the lot. The beauty around them suffices. The natural environment of this new house was so important to the owners that they—and the architect—designed a construction program that would protect even the smallest cactus on their property. Subcontractors were screened carefully by construction supervisor Chris Gans. The motto for the year-long construction was this: "It may look like a weed to you, but to the Barretts it's a precious plant."

The pool was built first—once the house was underway there would be no access to it. Rick Barrett, who served as general contractor, had a chain link fence placed around the property to form the construction envelope. There was only one entrance to the construction site for everyone, trucks included. "We wanted the house surgically installed," jokes the owner. He did direct the backhoe by identifying every tree and almost every shrub. From the street, the front door is reached by foot through the desert on a decomposed granite pathway that is almost imperceptible. The subcontractors did their jobs well.

Now that the project is finished the Barretts have only begun to experience all the advantages of their desert house. They've had a change in life-style—where they once went out a great deal, they now stay at home to watch the sky and desert. Their move has meant longer drives to work, but they use commuting time in the late afternoons to decompress from the day.

Although the porches will allow for entertaining of larger groups, the couple often have eight or ten people over for an outdoor barbecue. Many guests never come inside the house at all, but seat themselves on the wide concrete walls of the creek to watch the sunset when the walls of the Agua Caliente Canyon are lit with bright crimson.

The low-slung shapes of the contemporary Arizona ranch house fold into its desert setting, barely disturbing the fragile environment (LEFT).

Dawn tumbles into the rich Agua Caliente Canyon in northeast Tucson (RIGHT).

A cloudy desert sky is reflected in the pondlike pool that was designed by John Stropko of Tucson (LEFT).

White, night-blooming flowers top a *Carnegiea gigantea*, better known as the saguaro. The single waxy flowers, in view for a short time (usually in May), play a critical role in the survival of some of the flora and fauna of the Sonoran Desert (RIGHT).

Two completely different vegetation zones are found within twenty-five yards of each other on the site of the Barretts' new house. Along the creek, which has running water seven to eight months of the year, Arizona cottonwood trees, Arizona sycamores, ash, hackberries, and walnuts flourish. Up the slight incline to the house from the creek are found the plants of the dry desert—creosote bushes, mesquites, and the magnificent stand of saguaros. The owners have planted fifteen mesquite trees on the property near the sides of the house for privacy and have planted additional walnut, sycamore, and cottonwood trees near the creekbed. They will nurture the young trees until their roots can reach water, and then will leave them to the forces of nature.

The house is actually only thirty feet from the creek—and mornings here are like La Guardia Airport, say its occupants, when hundreds of desert birds pass through the property. Rick Barrett's teenaged son, a weekend occupant, has built four temporary dams along the creek to create little pools. On an island in the creekbed, the owners have set out a bench for picnics, and have even created a small volleyball court on a flat by the river. This is their private park, and they have seen white-tailed deer drinking at the creek and small horned owls quietly perched in the saguaros.

There is always a breeze tumbling down the canyon from the high country, and the Barretts can sit on the south-facing porch to listen to the calming sounds of the creek—as important to them as the natural vegetation. They have come home at last.

CALIF

At the turn of the century, there were few traditional rules in California governing landscape gardening—or governing much else for that matter. All who migrated to this land of dreams came with a lavishness of spirit that could not be tamed or worried by formal principles.

From the first Spanish explorers who named the state after a mythical land mentioned in a popular romantic novel, to the most recent newcomers seeking refuge from cold winters elsewhere, California has always represented magic—and a new start, where anything is possible. Those who work the soil—farmers and home gardeners—know this. Despite the state's largely semiarid nature, the availability of water and a temperate climate in many populated areas has allowed a subtropical garden of ginger and hibiscus to flourish within minutes of one displaying a spectacular array of cacti and succulents. Apples thrive here—so do oranges.

California's varied geographical regions have allowed its inhabitants to pursue their unique visions. There are rain-misted redwood forests in the north, skiable mountains in the central regions, and a spectacular stretch of beachfront property from north to south.

In southern California, the geography and the climate changes as one moves inland from the Pacific. Close to the ocean, the land is low, the temperatures moderated by the moisture-laden ocean air. Inland, the valleys and hills have hot summers and cool winters. The high mountains, such as the San Jacinto range near Palm Springs, are always cool in summer and frosted with snow in the winter months. Finally, in the central and eastern portions of southern California, the land is low, and gives way to the Mojave and Colorado deserts, and a portion of the Sonoran Desert coming up through Mexico.

The native flora segues easily from one geo-climatic region to another. Sage, fescue, and laurel sumac dominate the coastal regions, giving way to manzanita, California lilac, and chamisa farther inland. The pine-laden mountainsides provide a spectacular backdrop for the low deserts, populated by such exotic inhabitants as Joshua trees, ocotillo, and, in the desert canyons, native palms.

The first settlers of California were migratory Indians who displayed few agricultural tendencies. They built temporary shelters in areas where they fished, hunted, and gathered food. Beans from the mesquite tree, acorns, the heart of the spiny agave plant, and other plants, bulbs, and seeds were consumed for sustenance.

The Spanish missionaries were the first real farmers and landscapers of southern California, and their influence is felt even today in the crops still produced by the state and in the design of many houses and gardens. Led by the Franciscan missionary Father Junipero Serra, a cadre of soldiers, carpenters, ranchers, and missionaries trekked north from Baja California in 1769 and established twenty-one missions stretching from San Diego northward to Sonoma.

The Spanish padres brought with them primitive farming implements and a knowledge of irrigation techniques. They also carried precious seeds and cuttings of plants and trees that would transform their lonely outposts into agricultural Edens—and small replicas of their houses in Spain. Set in and around the protective adobe edifice of the mission itself, the gardens contained olives, grapes, and the first citrus planted in the New World. Pears, figs, pomegranates, dates, almonds, apricots, apples, and raspberries satisfied the sweet tooth; corn, beans, wheat, and lentils provided sustenance. Often, an herb garden was also cultivated, not only to provide flavors for cooking, but for

medicinal purposes as well. Surrounding the fields were rows of screening trees or huge banks of prickly pear cacti, to protect the crops from marauders.

Though the missionaries' work was hard and often not rewarding, they did manage to find time to express their aesthetic sensibilities through the planting of flower gardens and the thoughtful layout of the mission's inner courtyard. The flower gardens were often small due to scarce water resources. The fragrant Castilian rose, a symbol of Spain, was usually the centerpiece of the flowerbed, with hollyhocks, sweet peas, lilies, marigolds, larkspur, and other roses proffering blossoms that frequently became altar decorations. A small fountain was the focal point of the inner courtyard, which was often planted with shade trees, such as pepper trees and catalpa, and palms. Covered walkways, or portals, ran along the inner wings of the mission, and offered more cool spots for contemplation. The Spaniards also popularized the building of *ramadas*, or free-standing shade structures, which were planted with fast-growing, fragrant vines such as jasmine and passion vine.

In 1822, when Mexico declared its independence from Spain and claimed California as its own, the missions and their gardens became a part of history. The church land was divided up between favored ranchers, who had little or no interest in cultivation of anything that required tender nurturing. For the most part, the early ranchos consisted of an austere adobe house, devoid of shade trees or gardens, surrounded by vast acreage devoted to grazing cattle. The few Spanish/Mexican settlers who desired gardens had turned to the missions before their abandonment for cuttings and seeds. Additionally, the early settlers also made use of some native species, including

wild cherry, holly, California laurel, and Monterey cypress for shade, food, and decorative purposes.

During the early years of the nineteenth century, a handful of Anglo settlers began arriving in southern California, and copied the rough, adobe architectural style of the region. By 1850, California became a state, its quick acceptance accelerated by the discovery of gold in its mountainous regions. Miners and fortune-seekers piled into the state, followed by a more stable stock of pioneers, who spread south to what would become Los Angeles and San Diego. With the founding of gold, money and opulence became a way of life for some Californians. Gardens, too, became more decorative and showy than practical, with exotic plantings dragged across the plains from the East Coast or around Cape Horn via ship.

By the last half of the nineteenth century, the railroad reached California, linking it to the East. The railroad did a tremendous job in luring visitors to this land of never-ending summer. Their promotion men wrote glowing articles of the health-giving benefits of the California climate, and the railroads had lavishly landscaped hotels built at the end of the line, where a snow-weary Boston resident could step off the train and be surrounded by tennis courts, swimming pools, lavish gardens, and spectacular cactus displays. Many an Easterner with vague illnesses came west, making the hills of Los Angeles and the deserts of Palm Springs into vast sanatoriums.

Agriculture became a mainstay in the state's economy. Citrus, grapes (and raisins), olives, and other fruits were raised commercially in southern California; native flowering shrubs such as California buckwheat and sage were put to good use with bee colonies in the production of honey. In the desert near Palm

Springs, dates grew luxuriantly. Around the turn of the century, more exotic crops such as avocados and strawberries were grown in increasing abundance.

On the home front, transplanted Easterners had a bit of trouble adjusting to California's year round growing season. They had to learn that autumn in the Southwest is a time for planting, rather than preparing for winter's dormancy. Plants that the new settlers assumed were annuals could grow as perennials and bloom several times during the course of a year. The new settlers also had trouble adjusting to the concept of outdoor living. As opposed to the early Spaniards, who often took meals and refreshment out of doors, and used their courtyards, patios, and ramadas as fresh-air living rooms, the Anglo settlers clung to their old habits of socializing within their parlors, or at most, on the verandas of their Eastern-style houses. Their gardens became little more than decorative borders for the house itself.

Nurseries, however, sprang up around the state, cultivating plants for home use. Many of the nurseries' plantings were experimental and subtropical in nature; often, seeds and cuttings arrived from places as far away as Australia, South Africa, and South America. Many of the nursery owners were also the first professional landscape designers in southern California, and left their mark on entire cities. In San Diego, Kate Sessions was a pioneer horticulturist who ran a small flower shop and nursery from the late 1800s to about the 1920s. She planted the city's noted Balboa Park, creating a lush, shaded look that virtually characterized the city for decades.

During the first decades of this century, more money and people poured into the state. Oil was discovered in southern California. In and around Los Angeles, the movie industry grew, and those in the business wanted their houses to reflect their newly minted success. Landscape designers and architects were kept busy creating lavish gardens for vast estates; the clients were sophisticated and well traveled. A European, or Mediterranean, theme was popular, with vast stretches of lawns, formal pools, statuary, pergolas, and gazebos, all accented by large, dramatic trees. The landscaping talents of such notables as Florence Yoch, Lucile Council, Raymond Page, Ralph Stevens, A. E. Hanson, Katherine Bashford, and others were quite in demand during the first part of this century. Frederick Law Olmsted, Jr.'s, firm also had several projects of note in California, including the planning of the Palos Verdes estates near Los Angeles.

Ironically, as the population increased, so did the amount of land devoted to commercial agriculture. In addition to the avocado and strawberry crops that were relative latecomers to California produce, flowers became big business. Even today, fields of commercially grown flowers, shipped East during the winter months, can be seen in many areas of southern California.

The Depression and World War II put somewhat of a damper on exuberant garden design, but some very important trends emerged during this period in the life-styles of southern Californians. Homeowners, forced to stay put because of shortages and rationing, rediscovered their backyards; shortly after the war's end, the suburban boom began in earnest, and everyone wanted their own patio, barbecue grill, and swimming pool. Outdoor living was born again.

About that same time, California landscape architects Thomas Church and Garrett Eckbo managed to revolutionize garden design, leaving behind Beaux Arts principles and previously popular European influences. Though both were Harvard-trained, the landscape architects worked separately, but synchronistically. They matched residential landscape design to the steel, glass, and concrete forms of the new International Style of architecture; Eckbo and Church also played with the contours of the land, developing biomorphic forms with concrete terraces, pools, and walkways. Their "California School" of landscape design fathered the first kidney-shaped pools and redwood decks, built around existing trees in the garden. Said Eckbo in his book *Landscape for Living*, "Outdoors and indoors are inseparable. They are complementary and supplementary, two sides of the same door."

In recent years, the emphasis on the indoor/outdoor relationship has continued in southern California gardens. More amenities are being built into gardens, allowing people the pleasure of using their yards as "rooms" virtually year round.

Restoration and conservation have also come to the fore. Great gardens of California, such as some of those found in the old missions, are being replanted and studied for their historical importance. More and more, the plant palette is returning toward native species and drought-tolerant plantings in an effort to save precious water. Isabelle Greene, granddaughter of the Arts and Crafts architect Henry Greene, is noted for her water-saving designs in southern California. In Palm Springs, Patricia Moorten has been advocating the use of cacti and other desert plantings in home gardens since the late 1930s. Throughout California, more nurseries are cultivating sages, grasses, and other natives for use in residential landscapes.

Though today there may be more of a sense of thoughtfulness in California gardens, the exuberant spirit has not been lost. In California, the garden is still a place to dream.

Valley Palms

An Old-Style Palm Springs Garden

JUST A LITTLE more than a century ago, Palm Springs was a mere stretch of desert at the base of the towering San Jacinto Mountains, populated by the Agua Caliente band of Cahuilla Indians. These native peoples sought shelter from the summer's heat and the wind that swept through the valley in the cool, palm-lined canyons of the mountains, where streams flowed and hot springs invited medicinal soaks.

The Coachella Valley, in which Palm Springs lies, became known as a healthful oasis as early as the 1870s, when the Southern Pacific Railroad snaked its way through the nearby San Gorgonio Pass, en route to the Los Angeles basin. Anglo settlers began irrigating the land, planted date palms, citrus, and other crops, and touted the desert climate as an "absolute cure for all pulmonary and kindred diseases" in early real-estate advertising.

But an eleven-year drought, which began in the 1890s, put an end to these early developers' dreams; it wasn't until the 1920s that settlers came back to Palm Springs—this time in the form of Los Angeles and Hollywood stars in search of desert sun and respite from the pressures of city life. Resorts sprang

Protected by a clay tile roof, a gate signals the entry to the front yard and the house itself (LEFT). An earthquake in 1986 demolished the stacked stone garden wall and the gateway. It was rebuilt to meet modern building codes using the original stones to veneer an inner structure of cinder blocks.

The brilliance of the bougainvillea is offset by the delicate lantana blossoms (ABOVE). The color of the evergreen bougainvillea comes from three large bracts that surround its virtually microscopic flowers.

up to accommodate those with a passion for tennis, golf, and swimming. In what is now downtown Palm Springs, the elegant Desert Inn and El Mirador were considered to be the places to stay during the 1920s, thirties, and through the forties.

Approximately between the two hotels, Palm Springs' first subdivision, Las Palmas, was plotted, with the intent of attracting winter visitors to build gracious vacation houses. One such winter house attracted Palm Springs anesthesiologist Dean Berkus some sixty years after it was built. Berkus, then single, purchased the rustic stone house in 1984 because he was charmed by the mature landscape, the sweeping view of the mountains, and the peaceful, resortlike feeling prevalent in this older neighborhood. With his wife, Karen Berkus, a critical care nurse and a marketing representative at a nearby hospital, he has worked on some remodeling of the 3,000-square-foot house and on shaping up the once over grown yard.

From their research, the homeowners believe the house was built in 1922 as a winter retreat by the Schilling family of Los

The back portal is a newer addition to the house (ABOVE). The owner built it of lodge poles to complement the front portal. Hanging baskets of annuals and greenery help define the space.

Along the side of the house, a small patio off the master bedroom is a private spot for sunbathing and reading (TOP RIGHT). A flowerbed filled with multihued petunias and verbena frame the old palm tree trunks. The annuals in the beds and pots are changed twice a year, with heat-tolerant flowers such as vincas and zinnias planted during the summer and early fall. The wrought iron furniture is by O. W. Lee Company.

Informal barbecues and buffets take place on the back portal, where old-fashioned redwood picnic tables underscore the casual theme. (BOTTOM RIGHT).

The wrought iron sconce is original to the house (FAR BOTTOM RIGHT). In old-fashioned masonry terms, the rocks in the walls were once described as "one-man," "two-man," or "three-man" rocks to indicate how many workers were necessary to carry the rocks.

The front portal runs nearly the length of the house and is a cool locale for dinners or enjoying the sunset. Pots of aloes and miniature roses sit on the sunny edge of the portal. The vine along the roofline is a campsis, which bears a profusion of orange trumpet-shaped blooms in December and January. The decking material is flagstone (LEFT).

A cozy grouping of cushioned wrought iron furniture invites conversation and wine appreciation on the front portal. The window's wooden lintel was hand-hewn in the 1920s. Martha Washington geraniums and an arrangement of orchid tree blossoms add a fresh note to the setting. The furniture is by O. W. Lee Company (RIGHT).

A stepping-stone pathway leads from the front gate to the house's entry (FAR RIGHT). The lawn is winter rye, which is seeded over the summer's Bermuda grass when it becomes dormant in the autumn.

Angeles. Constructed in a straightforward ranch style, it has eighteen-inch-thick stone walls, topped by a clay tile roof. A sheltering portal, or covered porch, runs nearly the entire length of the front of the house. The same native rock used for the house's walls was used in constructing a garden wall, which defines the perimeters of the half-acre property. A gate, protected by a clay tile roof, signals the entry to the spacious front yard and to the house itself, which is set back on the lot. Inside, the high ceiling of the living room shows off the wooden beams, hand-hewn by Indian carpenters.

The Schillings lived in the house until the 1940s; it passed through several hands before the present owners acquired it.

During the years, there had been several additions made to the residence, including the conversion of the garage into a family room. A carport, blended discreetly with the style of the house, was added in lieu of the garage to one side of the adobe brick-paved driveway. An oval-shaped pool was built in the late 1950s, positioned in the vast green lawn of the front yard so that it commands an unobstructed view of the mountains. A new wall and fountain for the small backyard were built in the late 1960s.

Karen and Dean Berkus have continued updating the three bedroom house, carefully maintaining the charm of the old Palm Springs style. The garden has been the object of much pruning and replanting; the grounds are now restored to the cool, manicured oasis style of landscaping so popular in Palm Springs' early days, as a respite from the sun-drenched desert terrain.

Before their marriage, Dean Berkus tackled a few construction projects outdoors. He installed a gas barbecue in the backyard and built an open-beam shade structure of lodge poles for the back patio, in effect balancing the look of the front portal. Underneath the eaves of the front and back portals, a Micro-Cool misting system was installed. When it is turned on, a soft mist of chilled water is emitted from thin piping. The fine spray of cold water in the air lowers the temperature of the immediate area by as much as twenty degrees. This form of "outdoor air conditioning" makes life more comfortable, even during summer's intense, 110-degree-plus weather. The portals were also wired for music. Small outdoor speakers can be easily engaged when the couple entertains.

In 1986, an earthquake rattled loose the garden wall. The city condemned the old-fashioned stacked stone fence, and it had to be rebuilt to today's code, which meant using reinforced cinder

block as the main structural element, and facing the wall with the original rock as veneer.

When the construction projects were completed, Karen Berkus tackled the plantings. An avid gardener, she directed the removal of several trees that were crowding the setting. Because citrus is a hallmark of a classic Palm Springs garden, tangerines, pink grapefruit, Valencia oranges, and lemons were replanted in the front and back. Other trees, such as a purple-blossoming orchid tree, salt cedar, palms, and eucalyptus were shaped and pruned. Two *Ficus Benjamina*—one a relic from Dean Berkus' bachelor apartment—have flourished in the Palm Springs soil.

Where some of the trees were removed, Karen Berkus has carved out flowerbeds, which are filled with annuals twice a year. In the fall, after the summer's heat has ended, the beds—as well as many pots—are filled with petunias; primrose and cyclamen

grace the garden in the spring once the danger of frost has passed. Vincas and zinnias are hardy summer bloomers, and the geraniums seem to last all year. Karen Berkus waters the dozens of pots by hand, and in the summer, the watering is done on a daily basis.

Besides the annuals, there are other spots of color in the garden. A winter blooming campsis, or orange trumpet vine, has completely covered the posts and beams of the front portal, softly framing the house. Magenta-hued bougainvillea, pyrancantha shrubs with coppery-red berries, and pink-blossomed oleanders hug the garden walls. The rich green Bermuda grass lawn (over-seeded by rye in the winter months) is a cool foil to the garden's many colors.

Despite the coziness of the house, the owners often find themselves relaxing out of doors, particularly during the more tem-

On the street side, the house and garden are tucked behind a low native rock wall. Pyracantha, an evergreen shrub that bears copper-colored berries, grows up the sides of the walls; annuals, such as petunias, spark the flowerbeds below.

In the early morning light, a stand of palms is highlighted against the craggy peaks of the San Jacinto Mountains. The mountains, which rise to more than 8,000 feet in elevation, are frequently capped with snow in the winter months (ABOVE).

The swimming pool was built in the front yard in the late 1950s (TOP RIGHT). The carport, on the right, faces out onto a driveway and was built to complement the architecture of the main portion of the house on the left.

As seen from the front portal, the yard has a magnificent view of the nearby San Jacinto Mountains (BOTTOM RIGHT).

A grouping of *Washingtonia filifera* palms give the garden a sense of height (LEFT). Also known as the California fan palm, the trees are native to Palm Springs, favoring canyon stream areas as their natural habitat. Left untrimmed, the spent fronds become brown and hang down, covering the trunk.

Horizontal lines and vertical fissures mark the trunks of the *Washingtonia* palms (TOP RIGHT).

From the vantage point of the pool, the homeowners can watch the sun slip behind the San Jacinto Mountains (BOTTOM RIGHT).

perate spring and autumn months. They dine al fresco on the front portal, which they have furnished with peach-cushioned white wrought iron seating. In the back, they have purchased some old-fashioned redwood picnic tables, and here, they entertain friends with casual dinners of barbecued chicken or ribs.

They have had large groups at the house for outdoor parties. Friends come with swimwear and enjoy watching the sun slip over the San Jacinto Mountains from the cool vantage point of the pool; the front lawn is the perfect surface for a leisurely game of croquet or an energetic volleyball match.

For their April 1987 wedding, the couple hosted 200 guests at the house. The ceremony took place in the garden near the pool. A large tent for the dinner buffet was set up on the front lawn, and the guests circulated easily between the front and back portals and the tented area.

Most of all, the homeowners enjoy their house as the reminder of a gentler era. Sitting in the garden slows their modern-day pace. They can enjoy a glass of wine, watch their dogs chase one another on the grass, and feel the twilight gather on the desert town. If it's spring, the scent of orange blossoms is a heady perfume.

Even though the pressures of work are just a few minutes' drive away, the house and the garden are as calming as a stay in one of Palm Springs' fabled resorts.

Hilltop Contemporary

A House of Illusions in Palm Springs

O N THE ROCKY slopes of the foothills of the San Jacinto Mountains in Palm Springs, a road twists through the desert scrub past the handful of houses whose owners were bold enough to build on the steep mountainside. One of the houses is particularly beguiling.

Seen from below, the house is barely visible. Granite retaining walls—culled from the mountain itself—are frothed with massive, magenta-hued bougainvillea vines. Rising above the wall are wing-shaped, canopied shade structures; the crowns of dozens of palms rustle in the ever-present breeze. Through the vegetation, one can catch glimpses of the clean, contemporary lines of the house, which has antecedents in the spare International Style of architecture and in the work of Mies van der Rohe.

This hillside home, nicknamed the Bougain Villa, has been a restful oasis for Clara and William Burgess ever since they built the first portion of the house in the late 1950s. The couple has sought to blur the distinction between indoors and outdoors through the use of some pleasing architectural illusions and by furnishing the patio areas with as much care as the house's interior.

Set above Palm Springs, the house is perched on a shelf carved into the rocky mountainside. Pieces of granite culled from the site were used to create the retaining walls, capped by decorative arches. Bougainvillea grows profusely. Palms, primarily the stout *Washingtonia filifera*, or California fan palm, and the tall, slender *Washingtonia robusta*, or Mexican fan palm, tower above the contemporary house (LEFT).

From the hammock (ABOVE), one can see the tops of the property's palms. The low-voltage landscape lighting leads down the steps into the main yard and patio area.

Granite steps (LEFT) lead from the backyard up to a rocky site on the property, where a hammock offers a wide view of the city and valley below.

The back of the house is partially mirrored to reflect the rocky mountainside. The homeowners created a waterfall and a fish pond there to reiterate the landscape's oasis theme (TOP RIGHT).

A contemporary fiberglass and ceramic urn made by the San Diego firm Machado and the smaller, Korean rain jar flank the walkway from the driveway into the yard (BOTTOM RIGHT).

Like many from the Los Angeles area, the couple first came to this desert resort community in the Coachella Valley of southern California to escape the smog and enjoy sunning, swimming, and tennis. During one such vacation, William Burgess, who founded an electronics manufacturing firm, noticed a road running up the mountainside behind downtown Palm Springs. He was told that the road was built by prison laborers to connect a handful of lots that were never developed. Intrigued by the lots' views—and the fact that the hillside was free of the winds that regularly swept through the valley below—he purchased two adjoining lots with the intention of building a weekend retreat for his family.

Palm Springs architect Hugh Kaptur drew up the plans, based on the homeowners' designs. The house was small, simple, and situated on a shelf the homeowners had blasted out of the mountainside. The original design was not unlike Mies van der Rohe's noted Farnsworth House, built in rural Illinois—a flat roof extending into broad overhangs, with glass exterior "walls," that engage the homeowners with the natural surroundings.

However, the Burgess' design added some delightful twists to the glass-house concept. While the exterior walls are primarily glass (and sliding glass doors) where there are views, the back side of the house faces directly into the mountain. There, where the bedrooms are located, the couple chose to create some privacy with a stretch of solid wall, which is clad in mirrors on the exterior. Several sliding glass doors provide light for the bedrooms and access to the rear. When one walks through the narrow passageway between the rear of the house and the mountain wall, there is the cooling, enclosed feeling of being within a canyon due to the mirrors reflecting rock. To carry the mirror theme to the front of the house, an arched, mirrored fascia was added to the roof's overhang. Perlotta marble in a matte finish was used as the flooring indoors and was extended out around the pool in front of the house.

The original portion of the house, constructed between the late 1950s and early sixties, was 1,500 square feet. It contained a small kitchen, a cozy master suite, a bunk bed area for the two Burgess daughters when they were young, and a living room that had a boulder as one wall. Large pieces of granite from the preparation of the house's site were used to create retaining walls around the property, as well as to make a barbecue area toward the rear of the house.

Red cushions were made to match the dramatic canopy of bougainvillea vines above the barbecue (LEFT). At night, during informal dinners, barbecued lamb is often on the menu, and guests can enjoy the night breezes and city lights.

The stone barbecue pit and curving bench were built by Norwegian mason Olav Engum of granite culled from the site (ABOVE). Built between the side and back of the house, the barbecue area was used by the homeowners as their dining room for many years before the house was big enough to include space for an indoor dining area.

During those early years, the family spent every Saturday and Sunday at their hillside retreat. At that time, the only way to get to the house was to park on the street below and climb fifty stone steps, which meant quite a bit of exercise when carrying groceries, weekend supplies—or furnishings. The young girls enjoyed swimming and exploring the desert mountain. Because there was no dining room, Saturday evening dinners took place al fresco on the curved stone bench around the barbecue pit. The family loved the mild desert nights and the spectacular display of stars above the city lights.

Over the course of the years, the small retreat expanded and evolved, becoming more of a house where the Burgesses could entertain more formally. They acquired classic contemporary furniture, and their other collections of art grew as well.

On weekdays during the expansion, when the family returned to their Pasadena residence, Norwegian mason Olav Engum jackhammered more areas of the mountain so that the house and patios could be extended. He used the larger pieces of granite to complete the retaining walls and smaller pieces as fill behind the walls, thereby stretching out the level square footage surround-

Along one side of the house, a collection of classic Knoll International furnishings—including Mies van der Rohe's Barcelona chair—are grouped to create an outdoor living room (TOP LEFT). Upholstered in white and protected from the elements by a wide overhang, the furniture is an extension of the design theme used inside the house.

Near the entrance to the yard, a grassy promontory leads to a small patio, shaded by the sculptural expanse of the canvas and steel canopy (BOTTOM LEFT). The locale is perfect for watching the sun slip behind the San Jacinto Mountains. The terra-cotta urn is an antique Greek oil pot.

A small guest cottage with a roofline and architectural style echoing that of the main dwelling sits above it on a rocky plateau. The Italian urn has had the bottom removed and serves as a vent for the pool's heater (RIGHT).

ing the structure. The same Perlotta marble was used for the new, larger patios, including the main patio that wraps around the front and one side of the house. A second bedroom and bath were added, built around a rock outcropping that became a natural room divider. The living room was also expanded to include space for a dining area. A small guest house was constructed above the main house, and a spa was installed beside the pool. The homeowners also acquired an adjacent lot, using the extra space to build a much needed driveway and carport on the same level as the house.

With their daughters grown, Clara and William Burgess moved to Palm Springs permanently in 1974. Much of the expansion on the house and patios had been completed, allowing them to spend time with their collections, entertaining, and fine-tuning the landscape.

The yard is comprised of a simple palette of plant materials, chosen to create a cooling, oasis effect, which doesn't compete with the drama of the natural desertscape surrounding the property. San Diego Red and Barbara Karst varieties of bougainvillea add color with their fiery bracts, and shade is provided by a

Fibers from a palm frond, contrasted by the bright magenta hues of bougainvillea vine, are highlighted by the sun (RIGHT).

A small waterfall—one of three created on the property—and some smaller palms combine to form a grotto in a corner of the yard (MIDDLE RIGHT). The plant with the bulbous base is a ponytail, or bottle palm. The vessel is a contemporary piece, done by California artist Stan Bitters.

The trunks of old and young palms dwarf a jar from the Philippines (BELOW).

Near the entrance, the property's defining elements are revealed: palms, large urns, glass, mirrors, and canvas canopies (FAR RIGHT).

variety of palms—among them, the *Washingtonia filifera*, also known as the California fan palm, which is native to Palm Springs. Heat-loving vincas and asparagus fern rim the two small lawn areas just off the patios. A small citrus orchard is located just below the house.

The outdoor spaces provide many surprises. Three waterfalls behind and to the side of the main house were created to cascade down the face of the granite boulders. The water, circulated by pumps, collects in a series of ponds behind the house, which are home to graceful koi, gold comets, and other, smaller fish. The sound of the water is peaceful and cooling, even when the summer temperatures soar above 110 degrees.

The top of the tallest waterfall can be reached via a series of stone steps that twist up the mountain to the highest part of the two-acre property. There—another surprise: a rope hammock that invites rest and a relaxing view of the Coachella Valley. The hammock is hung beneath a wing-shaped canvas shade, stretched out on a steel frame. The canvas shade structure is one of several in the landscape, providing pleasant, filtered light for three seating areas. Designed by William Burgess and planned by neigh-

boring architect Albert Frey, variations of the shades also serve to delineate the main entry to the yard from the carport—and also serve as the carport itself.

Displayed within the landscape—and in the house's interior—are William Burgess' collection of large urns and hanging lamps. The collections started as alternatives to paintings, which could not be hung in the house because the walls were either glass or mirror.

Ranging in height from three to eight feet, the urns represent various time periods, artists, and nationalities. The acquisition of a contemporary ceramic jar by Henry Takemoto started the collection, but the more than sixty pieces now include a 300-year-old French water jar used on slave ships to Haiti, an olive oil urn from Spain, and a seventeenth-century Ching Dynasty porcelain jar that once contained a physician's herbs. The outdoor jars are firmly anchored to their sites; a bottomless Italian urn serves as the vent for the pool's heater.

Like the urns, the hanging lamps were collected by the homeowners on trips throughout the United States, Mexico, and Europe. A spectacular brass lantern from a Persian mosque

Many small dinner parties take place at the round glass table in the corner of the living room (LEFT). Sliding glass doors can be thrown open so that guests can enjoy the night air and the feeling of being outdoors. The turquoise-inlaid brass table base is the homeowners' design, crafted in Mexico. Lucite cubes are by Los Angeles artist Vasa; the rug is a Turkish antique.

A conversation area, sunken into an expanse of lawn, is a pleasant spot from which to view the city below (RIGHT). The eighteenth-century brass lamp is from a Persian mosque. A canvas shade structure pleasantly filters the bright desert sunlight.

The driveway and carport are relatively recent luxuries afforded to the homeowners. Prior to obtaining the adjacent lot upon which this access for automobiles was built, the family parked on the street below the house and climbed fifty steep stone steps up to the house. The carport and storage area were built with the same canvas and steel as the shade structures (FAR RIGHT).

illuminates one of the canvas-shaded conversation areas; some of the others are William Burgess' own designs. By night, the lamps provide dramatic pools of light throughout the landscape and within the house.

With their choice of furniture, the couple crossed the final barrier in making the indoor and outdoor spaces as one. As admirers of good twentieth-century design, they collected furniture by Charles Eames, Mies van der Rohe, as well as pieces by Eero Saarinen and Isamu Noguchi. Though the homeowners also have traditional patio furniture, they were not afraid to group their classics out-of-doors, on the covered patio, creating another living room. Indoors, pieces of similar lineage provide a visual link to the outdoors.

The house's layout has provided a very workable backdrop for entertaining. By night, the house becomes particularly dramatic. The pool lights, hanging lamps, and low-key interior lighting give off just enough illumination so that guests can find their way around, but still see the city lights.

Clara Burgess, involved in various California arts groups, has hosted benefit dinners at the residence. With larger groups, she often has the aid of a caterer, and tables of eight are set up on the two lawn areas and the patio. More often than not, entertaining means dinner for eight to ten guests. The round glass table in the corner of the living room is set, and lest anyone feel confined, the sliding glass doors are opened, instantly creating a formal, outdoor dining room. Informal family gatherings include swimming for the grandchildren and cookouts.

The couple's guest house is often occupied. Overnight guests often join the homeowners in an early-morning swim or a late-night soak in the hot waters of the spa. Breakfast and lunch are frequently loaded onto trays and enjoyed in the shade of one of the many seating areas. Visitors are always drawn out-of-doors by the views and the sunny climate; there is a reluctance to spend any time inside the guest house, no matter how cozy it is.

The house on the mountain also draws guests of an altogether different nature. A fox lives below the wall, and a bobcat occasionally comes down the mountain for a stroll in the yard. Raccoons make valiant attempts to snare the koi and comets, but the fish outsmart them by retreating to the deep center of the pond. Skunks, ring-tailed cats, roadrunners, and an occasional rattlesnake also put in appearances. But the Burgesses are more than happy to share their palm-shaded oasis with the local fauna.

Oceanfront Majesty

A Moorish Garden in La Jolla

I N THE 1920s, the village of La Jolla, just north of San Diego, was small, charming, and not quite engulfed in a real-estate boom. Gracious houses were built on generous lots, and were often designed in a cottagelike Craftsman style or in the Spanish Colonial Revival mode, with clay tile roofs and plastered walls. Southern California landscape design was in its infancy at the time, and gardeners struggled to tame the coastal landscape to create Mediterranean-style oases with plants that would tolerate the salt-laden winds. Around La Jolla's houses, the native sagebrush, cactus, grasses, and laurel sumac were replaced with palms, lawns, bougainvillea, hibiscus, and even roses, brought to the region originally as seeds and cuttings by immigrants who compared California's coastal clime to that of the coast of the Mediterranean Sea.

Despite the temperate climate, the concept of outdoor living—of creating a series of outdoor rooms that related to the house's architecture—was not prevalent in the 1920s, even in southern California. Though the houses of La Jolla were lovely and the gardens lush, one often had to traipse a long distance through the house to find a door to get to the garden.

Along the oceanside of the Spanish Colonial Revival-style house, the landscaping was kept simple to focus views on the Pacific. Natal plum, pittosporum, ice plants, and India hawthorn were used in the beds, as they could withstand the salt-laden winds. The raised terrace along the back of the house (LEFT) is a new addition, as are the French doors. The stairway on the left leads to a walkway that winds down to the beach; the steps on the right lead up to the spa and pool.

A giant Burmese honeysuckle softens the geometry of the oceanside terrace which is accented with Mexican *ollas*, or water pots, and a seated figure (ABOVE). When the sky is overcast, the ocean's color becomes a cool slate blue.

Such was the case with an oceanside residence now owned by Joan and Dennis Wise. The Wises, who enjoy the drama of the ever-changing sea, purchased the house in 1985 after it had been extensively renovated.

Built in 1928, the Spanish Colonial Revival house was one of the first in La Jolla to be built right on the bluffs overlooking the ocean. Situated on almost an acre, the house's three wings form roughly a U shape around a front yard, which faces a street; the back looks out over the water. Originally, the front yard was mostly lawn, punctuated by trees, and featured a fish pond. A rose garden took up much of a southern side yard, and the back had a small terrace and more lawn.

When the house was on the market in the early 1980s, it lacked many of the features that today's buyers want. The interior was gloomy and outdated; there were no good views of the ocean. None of the garden areas was easily accessible from the house, nor did they flow from one to another—each yard was virtually a dead end. Also, there was no patio large enough for outdoor entertaining on a very large scale, and no pool existed.

San Diego lighting designer John Case purchased the house in 1983 with the idea of making it over—both inside and out—so that it would fit current life-style needs and yet retain its beguiling twenties ambience. The designer asked Todd Fry, a La Jolla landscape architect, and Bruce Dammann, an architect from San Diego, to help him with the transformation.

While the "footprint" of the 7,000-square-foot house remained virtually the same, its interior was stripped down, modernized, and lightened by the addition of more windows and French doors that open onto various parts of the landscape. The den, located in the southern wing, was transformed into a "garden room" with the addition of French doors on one side that open onto the main courtyard, and sliding, mullioned pocket doors on the other side, which disappear into the walls and allow unobstructed views of and access to the small side yard.

The house was reroofed, and great pains were taken to remove and save the old red clay tiles. New roof tiles were layered in with the old to blur the distinction of age. A cactus sprouted out of one of the old roof tiles (probably brought there in seed form by a bird), and it, too, was carefully preserved.

In the garden, the landscape architect's job was to keep the property's original features, while adding modern amenities. Todd Fry chose a historical theme of Spanish gardens with

The large patio in the courtyard (TOP LEFT) can hold up to 100 guests for a sit-down dinner. Even when it's not in use, the patio's intricate paving patterns keep the space from looking too vast. The outdoor furnishings are a Brown Jordan style, dating from the 1940s.

A brick walkway connects the gatehouse to the front door (BOTTOM LEFT). A magnolia tree provides a sculptural element in the Moorish-themed courtyard; it is original to the property and was retained during the landscape remodeling. Dense, deep green baby's tears is used as the ground covering. Other plantings include azaleas and Australian tree ferns. The pot by the door is from Machado Designs, San Diego. The quatrefoil window above the entrance is typical of Spanish Colonial Revival architecture.

Low-growing India hawthorn shrubs delineate the walkway to the side yard. The steps lead up to the spa and pool, the site of a small rose garden before the landscape remodeling (RIGHT).

Stone rams' heads are the fountain element along the pool's back wall. Ferns and palms in the planter behind the fountain add to the lush, cool effect.

A special niche was created on the terrace for a bronze figure by Mexico City artist Virginia Aparisio (RIGHT).

On a clear day, the homeowners are able to see distant islands from their rear terrace (LEFT). The giant Burmese honeysuckle vine will eventually grow up the pillar and over the trellis roof structure. The two urns are *ollas*, or Mexican water pots.

A grassy promontory off the oceanside terrace is the only patch of lawn on the property. The wrought iron lantern is a custom design from Case Lighting Resources (ABOVE).

The oceanside terrace is often used for cocktail gatherings, small dinner parties, and viewings of the sunsets. The furniture is vintage Brown Jordan, handed down from the homeowner's grandmother (ABOVE RIGHT).

Australian tree ferns and a palm echo the textural interest of the clay tile roof (BOTTOM RIGHT).

Moorish influences because it fit comfortably with the architecture and the ambience of the La Jolla residence. Privacy, symmetry, and a sense of organization were the key elements in the old Moorish gardens, as were the cooling sounds of water and the repetition of patterns.

To maintain the property's historical integrity, many mature trees and plantings were retained in the new garden. A magnificent magnolia tree provides a sculptural element in the front yard, while a tea tree, a New Zealand Christmas tree, and many stately palms were respected as the elders of the landscape.

A new wall, presenting a serene face to the street, was built of plaster along the front and southern perimeters of the property; the garage and service wing of the house provides privacy to the north, and the yard is open to the ocean on the west. The expanse of the front wall is broken by the gatehouse, through which one enters the front courtyard and the house beyond. Layered plantings along the inside of the garden wall, such as Carolina laurel cherry, provide interest and texture. Young podocarpus, an evergreen tree, will eventually grow taller than the garden wall and block views of the neighbors' houses in this suburban setting.

One of the requirements in the landscape renovation was to create an area that could accommodate some 100 to 150 people for an outdoor party. To that purpose, the front lawn was removed and a courtyard patio that could withstand the rigors of large-scale entertaining was installed.

From the gatehouse, an unbroken walkway of large, terra-cotta-colored bricks leads through the courtyard to the front doorway. These bricks were also used as paving for the large entertainment area to the side of the walkway. The bricks were arranged in intricate patterns that give the impression of an Oriental rug. A Moorish motif of a rectangle, indented on the ends, is used for the large patio and two small paved areas, which are delineated by a row of gray cantera stone from Mexico.

Even when the patio is empty, the bricks and stone provide pleasing textural interest. The bricks were left unsealed so that they would age quickly. In addition, the Mexican stone is porous and has a tendency to become mossy in a short period of time, thereby blending the new materials of the landscape with the age of the house.

The front courtyard is readily accessible from the kitchen and dining room, making it easy to transport refreshments. A tile-topped bench surrounding the courtyard's fountain and another stretch of bench along one side of the patio provide informal seating areas.

Lush, green plantings in the front courtyard contrast with the warm rust and cool gray hues of the paving materials. A select color palette in the plant materials provides a neutral, serene look. Baby's tears is used as the ground cover that delineates the front walkway from the patios. Australian tree ferns, Alaska azaleas, and the orange-blooming Kaffir lily add further contrast to the courtyard. Established camellia shrubs near the house bloom white and pink.

Small rectangles of bricks, offset from one another, are the stepping stones from the front courtyard to the side yard, where the roses once bloomed. This sheltered area proved to be the ideal spot for the pool and spa, with easy access to the garden room and guest suite. The thirty-six-foot long lap pool repeats the Moorish indented-rectangle shape. It is plastered in a mottled gray shade,

On the pool patio, teak furniture by McGuire is finished in weathered gray to complement the tones in the pool and surrounding stone (ABOVE LEFT).

Terra-cotta-colored bricks and gray cantera stone from Mexico are the paving materials for the walkway and patios (ABOVE MIDDLE). Set off by baby's tears, Kaffir lilies, and azaleas, the bricks and stone were left unsealed so that they would age quickly.

Old Brown Jordan wrought iron furniture invites a tête-à-tête on the oceanside terrace (ABOVE RIGHT).

A bronze Oriental vase in the shape of a fish graces a bench on the oceanside terrace (LEFT).

giving the water a tranquil, pondlike quality, and is edged in the cantera stone. The spa is also plastered in gray and rimmed with the Mexican stone. Three stone rams' heads form the fountain element along the back wall of the pool. Ferns and palms behind the trough that feeds into the rams' heads intensify the cooling effect of the water.

Simplicity was the key element in designing the rear yard. Because of the spectacular views of the ocean, no trees or other obstructive plantings were used. A new tile- and brick-paved terrace, shaded by a pergola, was built along the entire length of the house, providing a smaller area for intimate dinners or cocktails at sunset. A niche was created for a bronze figure by Mexican artist Virginia Aparisio, and steps to the beach below were built. Ringing the small promontory of grass are wind- and salt-tolerant plants such as natal plum, ice plants, pittosporum, statice, and India hawthorn.

Other details for the garden were carefully thought out. The landscape lighting is extensive and dramatic. New copper lighting fixtures, copper gutters, and copper gutter pipes along the

213

The thirty-six-foot lap pool is plastered in gray to give the water a deep blue-black color. The pool, done in the Moorish-inspired, indented rectangle shape, is edged in cantera stone from Mexico (LEFT).

The homeowners installed a new seawall to stabilize the bluff upon which the house is sited (TOP RIGHT). The innovative wall tames the power of the waves, yet prevents the sand from being scrubbed away. The fiberglass strip at the top of the wall is a spray deflector.

A fountain, carved from Mexican cantera stone, is the soul of the Moorish-themed garden (BOTTOM RIGHT). The low wall around the water provides extra seating in the front courtyard; the Australian tree ferns add a tropical note.

house's roofline were treated with an acid finish to accelerate the natural verdigris patina. McGuire teak furnishings that weathered gray were chosen for the pool and spa area.

Joan and Dennis Wise had lived across the street from John Case's project for many years. They watched the renovation with interest, and, finally, purchased it when it was completed. Dennis Wise, a financial adviser, is a native San Diegan, and both he and his wife have an affinity for the sea. The house's siting and its newly created entertainment areas appealed to them.

Since they acquired the house, the couple has added personal touches to the property. They worked with San Diego interior designer Muriel Kinney to create an airy, traditional look for the house, incorporating many family heirlooms. A barbecue was built on the back terrace, adjacent to the sunny kitchen. Joan

Wise has planted roses and other vibrant flowers to add splashes of color to the landscape.

The main project the Wises tackled immediately was the construction of a seawall. Over the course of the decades, much of the original backyard was lost to the erosive forces of the ocean and wind. The bluffs were becoming steeper, and beachside caves were creeping farther inland, undermining the stability of the cliffs. When the couple first moved in, the storms produced breakers that shook the house; waves would cast surf spray and seaweeds over the roof of the house and into the sheltered front courtyard. They decided to take drastic action.

They asked Paul Benton, a San Diego architect, to help them with the project. Working with the California Coastal Commission and the Scripps Institute of Oceanography in La Jolla, he

came up with a novel, angled, articulated seawall that deflects the waves, yet keeps the sand from being scrubbed away. It took some fifteen months to build the seawall and the upper retaining wall for the backyard, as the construction could only take place at low tide. The caves were also filled in. The homeowners consulted with landscape architect Todd Fry to help them replant areas around the new walls.

With the major construction out of the way, the new homeowners often utilize the house's outdoor spaces. When they host smaller dinner parties of eight to ten people, the evening often starts with cocktails on the rear terrace, where all can view the distant Coronado Islands, navy ships on the horizon, or a spectacular sunset. The couple installed sea lights during the construction of the new seawall, and by night these powerful lights treat dinner guests to dramatic views of the waves and reefs. With larger gatherings (they have had as many as 200 people invited to a party), the front courtyard is tented for the guest tables, buffet, and band.

For the owners, the house is filled with simpler pleasures as well. The pool is heated year-round for swimming, and the day often begins with coffee on the master suite's balcony. Joan Wise tends a vegetable garden near the barbecue, where basil was the bumper crop one summer. Garden-fresh camellias floating in a crystal bowl are the signature decoration in the house.

The ocean and its life forms are riveting as well. At low tide, the steps down to the beach provide access to the teeming tide pools, filled with crabs, ghost shrimp, and anemones. The Wises keep binoculars handy to view the sea gulls, pelicans, sandpipers, and other sea birds; an occasional sea lion will bodysurf into view. November is lobster season, and many small fishing boats bob on the waters. In January, the whales pass by, heading for the warmer waters of Baja to winter. Though this particular stretch of La Jolla isn't known for its beach, hardy triathletes often swim by the Wises' home, training for upcoming competitions.

Now that they are living by the ocean, the couple's favorite time is when the sun slips into the ocean. When they can, they enjoy a glass of wine on the terrace and hope to see what some southern California surfers call the green flash, the mystical moment—when the conditions are just so—when the sun sinks below the ocean's horizon line and creates a prismatic green hue.

Coastal Retreat

A Lush Seaside Oasis in La Jolla

SOLEDAD MOUNTAIN is the highest point in the community of La Jolla, and although it rises only to some 822 feet above sea level, the views from its slopes are well worth the climb. To the north, west, and south, one can see the magnificence of the Pacific Ocean as well as portions of the La Jolla coastline.

In the 1920s, developer H. J. Muir discovered these same vistas and thought the western side of the mountain could become an alluring neighborhood for those who wished to be away from the hustle and bustle of La Jolla's downtown district. His "Muirlands" development, however, was slow to catch on. It proved to be too far from "The Jewel of the Sea," as La Jolla is often called, and remote from the city of San Diego to the south. There were problems with maintaining an adequate water supply, and by the 1930s, the Depression put a damper on property sales.

Ten years later the economy started to recover, and gracious family houses were being built within the mountainside development. In the 1940s, one such house was constructed on a corner lot by Hugh Baillie, president of United Press. Baillie and his wife, no doubt attracted to the area by the vistas

and fresh ocean breezes, built their house in a Monterey style, a derivative of the houses constructed by nineteenth century Anglo settlers of northern California. The architectural style blends Spanish and English Colonial detailing. The Baillies' house was two stories high, with two wings set in an L shape. The stuccoed house had a low-pitched roof and a balcony that ran along the second story of the bedroom wing.

During the ensuing decades, the house passed through several owners and was modified slightly to fit the fashions of the times. In 1986, the bougainvillea-covered house was on the market. A couple from New York was visiting the San Diego area, with thoughts of relocating their family to a more temperate climate. Inspired by its locale and the California weather, the couple purchased the house.

Immediately, however, the new homeowners realized the house—and the grounds—had to be modified to meet their specific needs. With four young children and two older ones who would be visiting regularly, there had to be plenty of room for games and activities, as well as privacy for the parents. The husband planned to work at home, so a quiet office space was needed as well.

The couple renovated the house and added a new wing, but the new construction was carefully planned to blend with the original architecture. Inside, lighter materials and more windows and French doors brightened the space. The old bedroom wing became the children's bedrooms, a playroom, and guest quarters. The new two-story wing parallels the former bedroom wing and contains a spacious kitchen and family room on the first floor, and a master suite and home office on the second. Balconies were added off the master bedroom and along the entire north side of the house. The newly renovated house forms a U shape, and, in the center, a new entry courtyard was established.

Large-scale furnishings, bright colors against neutral backgrounds, and contemporary art form the basis of the interior design scheme. From virtually every room of the house there is access to the outdoors.

During the course of the house's renovation, the grounds were remodeled as well. The old landscape was fairly simple—grass and trees. Though the house stands on a generous corner lot, the grassy yard originally sloped down from the house toward the street. There wasn't much level lawn area for children to play upon, nor was there a swimming pool or other recreational ame-

Weathered wooden doors and an old bench combine to create a pleasant entry into the front courtyard (TOP LEFT). Potted begonias, lushly growing bougainvillea, and a bottlebrush tree add red and pink hues to the setting. The paving material is adoquin stone from Mexico.

A multitrunked giant bird of paradise towers over the outdoor dining area just off the kitchen and family room (BOTTOM LEFT). Another tree with many trunks, the Mediterranean fan palm, leans over the back of the patio. Vividly colored tableware balances the brilliant flowers in the surrounding beds and containers. Furniture is by Bruce Eicher.

The forty-four-foot-long pool is marked for swimming laps—or doing some boating. The pool cover is stored at one end and rolls out automatically on tracks along the pool's edge. Standing guard over the water are king palms and a bronze figure, *Madre con nino en la cadera*, by the Mexican sculptor Zuniga (RIGHT).

nities as the Baillies belonged to a local tennis club when they built the house.

The new homeowners called upon landscape designer Michael Bliss of nearby Encinitas to help them develop the landscape for the children's activities, as well as for adult entertaining and relaxing. As transplanted New Yorkers, the family was also interested in creating a colorful garden, filled with plant material such as exotic palms and cactus, which would constantly remind them of their new locale.

Bliss first tackled the problem of the sloping yard. To create level land, the designer had a retaining wall built around a portion of the property and brought in some 100 truckloads of fill dirt for the area just off the kitchen wing and to the north of the house. The dirt was compacted to allow construction of a pool and spa in the side yard adjacent to the kitchen.

This pool area was designed to be convenient and self-contained. The rectangular, twenty-two by forty-four-foot pool was installed with an automatic pool cover that seals the water when it's not in use. Two built-in gas grills are set in a niche near the pool. A sink and refrigerator combine with the grills to create a

The stone horse head guarding the front door is one of a pair found by the homeowners during a trip to Mexico City (ABOVE LEFT).

Pink impatiens peek out from underneath the shade of Australian tree ferns in the entry courtyard (ABOVE).

The northern side of the garden has a large expanse of grass for children's games and entertaining. The flowerbed, filled with impatiens and cosmos, is shaded by a tall star pine. More impatiens—this time in hanging baskets—grace the balcony, which was added when the house was remodeled. The baskets are watered via a narrow pipeline that runs along the roofline; water from the baskets drains into the grass below (RIGHT).

The chimney, with its tile roof and arched vents, was given architectural character during the remodeling. A hanging basket planted with impatiens and bougainvillea soften the lines of the house (LEFT).

A water lily floats serenely in the pond surrounding the courtyard's fountain (TOP RIGHT).

A variety of the pink chrysanthemum is a lively accent flower for the beds and containers near the pool (FAR TOP RIGHT).

The densely packed echeveria's rosettes are more clearly defined in the late afternoon sun. The succulent spreads freely by offsets (BOTTOM RIGHT).

The sago palm, planted near the pool, is actually not a palm at all, but rather a primitive conifer. The cone bursts with seed in the autumn. A hardy impatiens has grown up through the plant's featherlike leaves (FAR BOTTOM RIGHT).

A spiral staircase leads from the garden to the balcony and the second-story office (LEFT). Below, a flowerbed filled with impatiens and bird of paradise hugs a walkway.

Geraniums, ringed with purple lobelia, make a strong color statement on the pool patio (TOP RIGHT).

A *Cereus monstrosus*, or brain cactus, is a striking specimen found at a Malibu nursery. Surrounded by agaves and other cacti and succulents, it makes a sculptural entry piece near the front courtyard (BOTTOM RIGHT).

compact outdoor kitchen. A bathroom and outdoor shower are located to one side of the spa. Mexican adoquin stone is the paving material around the pool and spa, where the patio is wide enough to accommodate chaises, lounge chairs, and outdoor dining furniture.

For the front of the house, the homeowners and landscape designer created a grand new entrance. Custom-designed wrought iron gates recess automatically behind the garden wall to allow cars up the semicircular drive, surfaced with charcoal-colored Bomanite, a decorative paving material. A short flight of stairs leads up to a set of weathered wooden doors that open up into the entry courtyard, which is anchored by a fountain set into a raised koi pond. The house's front doors are similar to those of the courtyard.

Just outside the children's wing, the small yard space was developed into an innovative playground. A paved sidewalk loops around the side yard, providing the perfect pathway for tricycles, bikes, and skateboards. A multilevel playhouse is set on a thick, springy base of rice hulls, to cushion falls. A sandbox, small theater for puppet shows and "live" acts, and a basketball hoop are among the other carefully planned amenities for the children and their friends.

A large expanse of lawn takes up most of the north portion of the property. Although it's adequately sized for throwing a football or playing a bit of soccer, the grassy area is serene and simple in contrast to the more developed areas of the landscape.

One tree was lost during the construction of the new semicircular drive and entrance, but a conscious effort was made to save as much of the property's mature vegetation as possible. The front courtyard's huge bougainvillea—grown to small tree size after forty years—was carefully nurtured, as was a strawberry tree near the kitchen door and a stand of star pines along the northern edge of the yard.

To enrich the look of the landscape and to maintain the property's 1940s ambience, many more mature trees and plants were added, mostly in the form of palms and cacti. The owners became very interested in the selection of the garden materials and traveled throughout the state in search of specimen plantings. Their diligence yielded treasures such as a set of tall, boxed palms purchased from the film studio Twentieth Century Fox, which had been moved for decades from movie set to movie set as background trees. They were "liberated" from the boxes and

planted outside the house's garden wall. A huge, gnarled brain cactus was found crated up in a nursery in Malibu after the original buyer backed out of the purchase. It was positioned in a bed filled with cactus and succulents near the entry to the courtyard. A twenty-trunked Mediterranean fan palm was another discovery that wound up near the pool. A crane was rented to position the new trees.

The smaller plantings were also carefully considered. A lush, subtropical look was the theme for the entry courtyard. Australian tree ferns, pigmy date palms, and bird of paradise rim the courtyard's adoquin stone patio. Water lilies float lazily in the fishpond. Flowerbeds filled with impatiens and daylilies ring the north-side lawn and pool area; a statue of a mother and child by the Mexican sculptor Zuniga stands proudly against a backdrop of sago palms and potted impatiens. Gardener Eduardo

Osuna keeps pots filled with ruellia, geraniums, marigolds, sweet William, begonias, chrysanthemums, pansies, alyssum, and fuchsia for brilliant splashes of color against the quiet green of the rest of the garden.

After nine months of remodeling and planting, the landscape looks as though it has been there since the 1940s. The owners immediately put it to good use. The children practice their swimming almost year-round, and the play area is usually abuzz with young energy. The couple entertains often. Family and friends gather for one of their gourmet dinners served al fresco, or for an informal barbecue. Even during work hours, the husband is not isolated from the refreshing beauty of the garden. Through a large window in his second-story office, he can see the flowers below, hear the palm fronds rustling in the breeze, and watch the sky melt into the ocean in the distance.

A decades-old bougainvillea makes a canopy over the doorway into the house (FAR LEFT). The door handles are a custom design from San Diego Wrought Iron. Water lilies and other plants provide the koi with hiding places in the courtyard's fishpond.

Rhapis, or lady palm, and bougainvillea reach to the clay tile roof over the house's front doorway. Hanging baskets of fuchsia create a spectacular display along the balcony (LEFT).

227

Canyon Vista

A Native Landscape Atop San Diego

I

N THE EARLY 1900s, the city of San Diego began to spread beyond its bayside setting. To the north and east, small suburban developments began to spring up on top of mesas, separated from one another by brush-filled canyons. Street car lines snaked their way from downtown into these neighborhoods, creating southern California's first generation of commuters. To compensate for the hilly geography, small footbridges were built over the canyons so that denizens could walk easily to a trolley stop or into another neighborhood.

Normal Heights was one such neighborhood that flourished above downtown San Diego in the early part of the century. Its bungalows and modestly scaled Spanish Revival houses were built along jacaranda-lined curving streets that followed the contours of the canyon's edge. Construction there reached a peak in the 1920s and thirties; by the end of World War II, Normal Heights was considered to be part of the city itself. Young families migrated farther into the outlying suburbs during the ensuing decades, and the neighborhood began a gentle decline. In the 1970s, however, interest in the area revived. Normal Heights' proximity to the city's center was once again a draw, as was

A section of the roofline telescopes the lighthearted blend of Mission Revival, Art Deco, and Southwestern styles of architecture (LEFT).

Deeply recessed windows allow a controlled amount of light to enter the hallway of the guest/study wing (ABOVE).

The architectural theme of squares, arches, and ziggurat shapes is readily apparent at the front of the house. The arch in front of the garage helps to minimize its impact, while the tile-roofed entry pavilion creates a sense of ceremony upon walking into the front courtyard. The washed coral stone driveway is softened with a center strip of grass. The owners, active in the California Native Plant Society, chose to landscape their property with many local species, such as the California wax myrtle by the garage's arch (LEFT).

Viewed from across the canyon, the rear of the house is a pleasingly eclectic blend of architectural motifs (ABOVE). The small yard space is sheltered from the ever-present canyon winds by the glass garden wall on the right.

the abundance of older houses with architectural character. Many young people and families began to buy and renovate the small houses.

In 1976, Lois and Richard Miller bought a 1,600-square-foot Spanish Revival house in Normal Heights. Having recently moved to California from the East, they liked the house's canyon-side locale (part of their narrow, half-acre lot descends to the bottom of the steep canyon itself) and the charm of its 1921 architecture. During the course of the next few years, the couple fixed up the house and redid the upper portion of the backyard closest to the house to include raised vegetable beds, a tiled patio, and a hot tub. They left the canyon in its natural state, a hillside filled with native chamise, prickly pear cactus, lemonade berry, laurel sumac, and manzanita.

During the summer of 1985, disaster struck. A brush fire spread from a nearby canyon into the one by Normal Heights. Lois Miller, who was home at the time, watched in disbelief as the flames rushed toward their street. She evacuated the house, taking the dog and a few personal belongings with her. When the couple returned to the site the next day, they saw that theirs was

231

one of some seventy houses destroyed by fire. In the long run, however, it proved to be an opportunity.

Lois Miller, the director of land use planning for a large corporation, was also the president of their neighborhood association. She and her husband, a state park ranger, were determined to stay and rebuild on their property. The burned section was declared a federal disaster area, and during the next months, Lois Miller became a community activist, helping her neighbors cut through red tape and helping them rebuild their houses as well.

The couple salvaged what little was left of their possessions—some photograph albums, a few books, a collection of vintage pottery—and began thinking about the ideal house for the site. While they liked their old house, it hadn't addressed the canyon views (a garage set in the backyard partially blocked the vistas), nor did it really fit their indoor/outdoor life-style. Therefore,

they opted not to rebuild on the existing foundation. By the time they met with San Diego architect Marc Tarasuck, they had a rough idea of what they wanted.

The architect agreed that the house should be modest in scale, given the fifty-foot-wide lot, and that it should pay homage to the street's former 1920s vernacular. The couple wanted a simple, contemporary floor plan, an entry courtyard, and a light-filled house that was private to the street, yet would capture the magnificent canyon views.

Tarasuck, along with his partner, architect Tedd Foley, created a 1,963-square-foot house that blends Mission Revival, art deco, and native Southwestern schools of design in a lighthearted, contemporary manner. The playful architecture of the melon-hued house is based on a theme of arches, squares, and ziggurat shapes; teal is used as the trim color.

Set around an enclosed front courtyard, the house is comprised of three sections. The central section of the house is roughly square; its two-story height is minimized because it is set back from the other two wings. This main section is comprised of a small foyer, a great room, which contains the living and dining area, both simply furnished with contemporary pieces, and an open kitchen. Up the stairs is the master suite. Flanking the central core of the house is a one-car garage and a single-story wing containing the powder room, study, and guest quarters.

Visitors enter the front courtyard and house from the street through a ziggurat-shaped metal gate, located in a tile-roofed gatehouse. To one side of the gatehouse, a large decorative archway over the drive softens the impact of the garage. Clay tile was also used as the roofing material for the stairwell's tower in the main section of the house; metal-edged parapets in the Mission

Teal-trimmed windows, decorative tiles, and an arch-capped chimney pay whimsical homage to the neighborhood's former 1920s vernacular (FAR LEFT).

The front courtyard, paved in Spanish Catalan tile, is spacious enough for outdoor entertaining. A small fishpond is a refreshing sight along the garage wall at left. Potted flowers can be shifted as the mood strikes, and add interest along the wall of the guest wing. The central tower houses the staircase to the master suite (MIDDLE LEFT).

A lone San Diego Red bougainvillea is a shock of color near the front door. The pots contain dusty Miller and marguerite (ABOVE LEFT).

The gatehouse (ABOVE) creates a sense of drama and enclosure, heightening the feeling of spaciousness in the front courtyard. The black metal gate reiterates the square and ziggurat-shape theme. The mailbox is clear glass on the other side of the column, allowing the owners to see from a distance whether the mail has arrived.

Revival motif add decorative interest in other portions of the roofline. In addition to the teal window surrounds, teal ceramic tiles are used in decorative patterns along some of the expanses of stuccoed walls.

As much as the couple planned to enjoy their new house and its serene interior, they also intended to spend a good deal of time outdoors, gardening and enjoying the temperate climate. With that in mind, the house's exterior spaces were carefully detailed. The architect and homeowners worked with landscape architect Andy Spurlock to devise a master plan for the front courtyard and small backyard.

The front courtyard, paved in Spanish Catalan tile, has small beds for flowers and plants, and a koi fish pond along one wall. The pond's shape echoes that of the arched roof parapet above it. Seating is provided by vivid turquoise Italian garden chairs. The guest bedroom has access to the front courtyard via a pair of French doors.

A gate behind the garage leads to a path, lined in redwood bark, which winds past a vegetable garden in the narrow side yard and into the backyard. A raised terrace, just off the dining

area of the great room, is sheltered by a pergola of rustic wood. From the bent twig chairs that furnish the terrace, there is a sweeping view of the backyard and canyon beyond. Another tiled patio area rims the canyon's edge, and here a rustic table and chairs create an outdoor dining room. Because the canyon-top locale is rarely free of wind, Tarasuck designed a glass garden wall that zigzags in and out along the edge of the backyard, protecting the occupants, yet not blocking the views. Below the glass wall, a short set of stairs leads down to a narrow trail into the canyon.

The owners chose to landscape their garden with native California species, creating a garden that requires little maintenance and, more important in an arid region, little water. The planting efforts have been somewhat experimental; the interest in gardening with native plants is just dawning in the San Diego area. With few local nurseries carrying native plants, Richard Miller traveled as far north as the Los Angeles area to obtain good specimens.

The Millers had their garden's local hard clay soil removed and refilled with lighter, more arable soil, amended with organic

French doors lead from the guest room to a private corner of the front courtyard. The chairs are Italian (FAR LEFT).

A weathered table and hand-painted chairs create an inviting setting for afternoon tea near the sheltering garden wall. Below, the canyon is beginning to regreen after a devastating brush fire. Table items are Pacific Pottery and Fiestaware; the snake is a Mexican folk art piece (MIDDLE LEFT).

The rear pergola, built by the owner, provides a sense of shelter for the terrace off the dining room (LEFT). The bent twig chair adds a rustic note. In the flowerbed, agapanthus and begonias share space with spring bulbs. The grass is "Jaguar," a turf-type fescue that is drought-tolerant.

235

material. Some plants flourished, others did not. Those that did survive provide the landscape with subtle color through their greenery and blossoms, and interesting textures. Near the street and in the front courtyard, ceanothus (also called wild lilac) blooms bluish-purple in the spring, as does a variety of silvery-leafed sage. Lavatera, which has pink-purple blossoms resembling a single hollyhock, makes a spectacular display just inside the front gate. California wax myrtle, California buckwheat, and flannel bush are also woven throughout the front and back gardens of the house. The Millers replanted some low-growing native species down into their part of the canyon, letting nature—and time—heal most of the fire's scars.

Their landscape also includes some domesticated plantings, such as bougainvillea and pots of annuals. In the side yard, a fledgling orchard produces Dorsett Golden and Anna apples, adapted to the desert climate, as well as lemons, limes, and apricots. The owners installed a small strip of turf near the street to keep the front yard in sync with the neighborhood, and they also placed a corner patch of turf in the backyard where their dog can romp. A narrow strip of grass runs up the center of the driveway, a

The terra-cotta sun is from Puerto Vallarta, Mexico (TOP LEFT).

The lavatera, or tree mallow, is native to the Channel Islands off the southern California coast. The blossoms can range from deep magenta to almost white (BOTTOM LEFT).

A tile-topped column is an impromptu work space for trimming florist's flowers (ABOVE).

A cedar pelican, carved by a Washington oyster grower during the off-season, was one of the few yard accessories to survive the fire (RIGHT).

In the corner of the back yard, the bent twig chair is perfectly positioned to monitor the return of the birds to their canyon nesting areas, as well as the silvery movement of the distant freeways' traffic. The bicycle weathervane, another survivor of the fire, monitors the wind patterns (FAR RIGHT).

a 1920s-era landscaping device that breaks up the continuos expanse of the paved surface.

The house garnered an award for the architect from the local chapter of the American Institute of Architects. But for the Millers, the house has given them rewards—many of which are intangible. For one, the house—both indoors and out—works for their busy life-style. It is an easy place in which to entertain. For large groups, the couple sets up a bar and buffet table in both the front courtyard and backyard, and guests circulate throughout the house's main level and the outdoors. With the dining area's French doors thrown open to the backyard, any dinner party, big or small, can feel part of the outdoors.

When it's just the two of them, the couple can enjoy a sunset over the canyon and distant, shimmering freeways (a viable piece of southern California culture) from the raised terrace. With binoculars, they watch the return of the birds to their regreening canyon habitat. Produce from the organic vegetable garden finds its way into many speciality dishes, and the fruit is eaten fresh or canned. The extra-wide garage provides plenty of elbow room for building projects; a skylight and sliding glass doors at one end give the space light and a view of the canyon.

Most of all, however, the homeowners are glad to be back in their historic neighborhood, in a house that's even better suited to their love of the outdoors.

238

SOURCES

Architectural Materials

**ATASCADERO/MEXICAN
TILE COMPANY**
2222 East Thomas Road
Phoenix, AZ 85014
(602)954-6271
and
1148 East Broadway
Tucson, AZ 85716
(602)622-4320
Tile, architectural remnants, accessories.

**GUADALAJARA
FOUNTAINS**
1102 East Indian School
Road
Phoenix, AZ 85014
(602)277-5262
Hand-carved fountains and outdoor furniture.

MELLUZZO STONE CO.
1965 East Beardsley
Phoenix, AZ
(602)867-9000
Landscaping stone and boulders.

**PROGRESSIVE CONCRETE
WORKS**
1102 West Hatcher Road
Phoenix, AZ 85021
(602)943-7241
Suppliers of Bomacron, paving material used for McGillicuddy residence, Carefree, Arizona.

Furnishings and Accessories

**AMERICAN COUNTRY
COLLECTIONS**
620 Cerrillos
Santa Fe, NM 87501
(505)984-0955
Chairs, Kelly residence, Santa Fe, New Mexico.

BROWN JORDAN
8687 Melrose
Los Angeles, CA 90069
(213)659-0771
Outdoor furnishings.

BRUCE EICHER
8755 Melrose
Los Angeles, CA 90069
(213)657-4630
Rust-finished outdoor furniture, Houston residence, Taos, New Mexico

**HOME DECORATOR
FABRICS**
3200 East Grant
Tucson, AZ 85716
(602)327-2824
Willow chairs and cushions, Barrett residence, Tucson, Arizona.

**HOUSE 'N GARDEN
FURNITURE**
4310 East Broadway
Tucson, AZ 85711
(602)327-5675
Glass-topped table, Barrett residence, Tucson, Arizona.

McGUIRE
151 Vermont Street
San Francisco, CA 94103
Outdoor furniture, Wise residence, La Jolla, California.

PARTRIDGE CO.
131 Bent Street
Taos, NM 87571
(505)758-1225

REED BROTHERS
Turner Station
Sebastpol, CA 95472
(707)795-6261
Carved redwood furniture.

TROPITONE
5 Marconi
Irvine, CA 92714
Outdoor furnishings.

Galleries, Artists, and Craftspeople

CLAIBORNE GALLERY
558 Canyon Road
Santa Fe, NM 87501
(595)982-8019
Antique table, Hitchcock residence, Tesuque, New Mexico.

GLENN GREEN GALLERIES
6000 East Camelback Road
Scottsdale, AZ 85257
(602)990-9110
and
50 East San Francisco
Street
Santa Fe, NM 87501
(505)988-4168
Representing sculptor Allan Houser.

CHRISTOPHER HEEDE
7007 East Rancho Del Oro
Drive
Cave Creek, AZ 85331
(602)488-2630
Ceramic pieces, McGillicuddy home, Carefree, Arizona.

Landscape Architects, Landscape Designers,
Contractors, Architects, and Interior Designers

**ELAINE HORWITCH
GALLERIES**
129 West Palace
Santa Fe, NM 87501
(505)988-8997
Also locations in Scottsdale
and Sedona, Arizona, and
Palm Springs, California.
*Folk art animals, Hitchcock
residence, Tesuque, New
Mexico*

SUSAN HARRISON KELLY
Santa Fe, NM
(505)982-8682
*Artwork, Kelly residence,
Santa Fe, New Mexico*

JIM WAGNER
131 North Pueblo Road
Taos, NM 87571
(505)758-9017
Hand-painted furniture.

**JAMES ABELL, AIA
JAMES ABELL &
    ASSOCIATES**
2 West Alameda Drive
Tempe, AZ 85282
(602)968-3023
*Architecture and land-
scape architecture.*

**MICHAEL BLISS
MICHAEL BLISS &
    ASSOCIATES**
221 Sunset
Encinitas, CA 92024
(619)753-8261
*Landscape designer for La
Jolla, California,
residence.*

**MARCUS BOLLINGER
LANDSCAPING BY ANDRE**
10830 North 71st Place,
Suite 205
Scottsdale, AZ 85254
(602)483-8088
*Landscape designer for the
McGillicuddy residence,
Carefree, Arizona.*

**JOHN CASE
THE CASE COMPANIES**
969 Buenos Avenue
San Diego, CA 92110
*Lighting design and re-
modeling for Wise resi-
dence, La Jolla, California.*

**DANIEL R. ELDER, ASLA
ROCK CREEK STUDIO**
8765 East Bear Place
Tucson, AZ 85749
*Landscape architect for
Stilb pool, Tucson, Arizona.*

EL TROS COMPANY
Jeremiah Buchanan
Ranna Wiswall
Box 5745 Upper Tros
Taos, NM 87571
(505)758-2158
*Adobe restoration of
Buchanan/Wiswall resi-
dence, Taos, New Mexico.*

ALBERT FREY, FAIA
Palm Springs, CA
(619)325-2851
*Architectural planning for
shade structures, Burgess
residence, Palm Springs,
California*

TODD FRY, ASLA
La Jolla, CA
(619)459-8005
*Landscape architect for
Wise residence, La Jolla,
California.*

**VICTOR JOHNSON
JOHNSON NESTOR MOR-
    TIER & RODRIGUEZ**
343 West Manhattan
Santa Fe, NM 87501
(505)983-5497
*Architect for Santa Fe, New
Mexico, residence.*

**HUGH KAPTUR, AIA
KAPTUR & CIOFFI**
700 East Tahquitz Way,
Suite E
Palm Springs, CA 92262
(619)325-1557
*Architectural planning for
Burgess residence, Palm
Springs, California.*

TERRY KILBANE, AIA
P.O. Box 997
Carefree, AZ 85377
(602)998-1779
*Architect for Carefree, Ari-
zona, residence.*

RICK KLEIN
Box 85
San Cristobal, NM 87564
*Garden design and mainte-
nance for Houston resi-
dence, Taos, New Mexico.*

**STEVE MARTINO, ASLA
MARTINO & ASSOCIATES**
7550 East McDonald Drive
Scottsdale, AZ 85253
*Landscape architect for
Carefree, Arizona,
residence.*

FRANK MASCIA, AIA
CDG Architects
345 East Toole Avenue #202
Tucson, AZ 85701
(602)629-9752
Architect for Barrett residence, Tucson, Arizona.

BAKER H. MORROW, ASLA
MORROW & COMPANY,
**   LTD.**
210 La Veta NE
Albuquerque, NM 87018
(505)268-2266

DONALD RANDOM
**   MURPHY**
Santa Fe, New Mexico
(505)984-0236
Interior designer for Houston residence, Taos, New Mexico.

JUDITH PHILLIPS
BERNARDO BEACH
**   NATIVE PLANT FARM**
1 Sanchez Road
Veguita, NM 87062
Landscape designer.

WALTER E. ROGERS
ACACIA GROUP
325 South Euclid #113
Tucson, AZ 85719
(602)622-2302
Landscape architect.

RON ROBLES
Santa Fe, NM
(505)988-7040
Designer for Fillini/Robles home, Santa Fe, New Mexico.

JEFFREY STONE, ASLA
7534 La Jolla Blvd.
La Jolla, CA 92037
(619)459-3414
Landscape architecture.

JOHN STROPKO
THE NEW DESERT
**   GALLERY**
P.O. Box 41675
Tucson, AZ 85717
(602)326-4992
Designer and pool contractor for Barrett pool, Tucson, Arizona.

MARC TARASUCK, AIA
TARASUCK-FOLEY AND
**   ASSOCIATES**
744 G Street, Studio 206
San Diego, CA 92101
(619)262-0100
Architect for Miller residence, San Diego, California

WALTER ANDERSEN
**   NURSERY**
3642 Enterprise Street
San Diego, CA 92110
(619)224-8271

ARIZONA NATIVE PLANT
**   SOCIETY**
P.O. Box 41206
Sun Station, Tucson, AZ
    85717

BERNARDO BEACH
**   NATIVE PLANT FARM**
1 Sanchez Road
Veguita, NM 87062
Write for plant list; a local source only.

CALIFORNIA NATIVE
**   PLANT SOCIETY**
909 12th Street
Sacramento, CA 95814

DESERT TREE NURSERY
18610 North Cave Creek
    Road
Phoenix, AZ 85024
(602)569-1300
Specializing in Sonoran and arid-region plants.

DESIERTO VERDE
Several Arizona locations.
(602)820-2970
Specializing in desert trees and shrubs.

GREENWORLD GARDEN
**   CENTERS**
Several Phoenix-area
locations.
(602)437-0700.

NATIVE PLANT SOCIETY
**   OF NEW MEXICO**
P.O. Box 5917
Santa Fe, NM 87502

NATIVE SEEDS/SEARCH
2509 North Campbell Avenue, #325
Tucson, AZ 85719
(602) 327-9123
Preservation and information about Southwestern seeds and plants.

NEEL'S NURSERY
3255 East Palm Canyon
Palm Springs, CA 92264
(619)327-1251

OASIS
2719 East Broadway
Tucson, AZ 85716
(602)325-9811

	Organizations	Public Gardens	Publications

PLANTS OF THE SOUTHWEST
6670 4th Street NW
Albuquerque, NM 87107
(505)344-8830
and
930 Baca Street
Santa Fe, NM 87501
(505)983-1545

RANCHO SOLEDAD NURSERY
18539 Aliso Canyon Road
Rancho Santa Fe, CA 92067
(619)756-3717

SHEPARD IRIS FARM
3342 West Orangewood
Phoenix, AZ 85051
(602)841-1231
Desert-adapted iris bulbs.

NATIONAL XERISCAPE COUNCIL, INC.
8080 South Holly
Littleton, CO 80122

SANTA FE GARDEN CLUB
Santa Fe, NM
(800)338-6877 (Tour information only)
Club presents "Behind the Adobe Walls" home and garden tours each July and August.

ARIZONA-SONORA DESERT MUSEUM
2021 North Kinney Road
Tucson, AZ 85743
(602)883-2702

BOYCE THOMPSON SOUTH-WESTERN ARBORETUM
P.O. Box AB
Superior, AZ 85273
(602)689-2811

DESERT BOTANICAL GARDEN
1201 North Galvin Parkway
Phoenix, AZ 85008
(602)941-1225

THE LIVING DESERT
47—900 Portola Ave.
Palm Desert, CA 92261
(619)346-5694

MOORTEN BOTANICAL GARDEN
1701 South Palm Canyon Drive
Palm Springs, CA 92264
(619)327-6555

QUAIL BOTANICAL GARDENS
230 Quail Gardens Drive
Encinitas, CA 92024
(619)436-3036

TOHONO CHUL PARK
7366 Paseo del Norte
Tucson, AZ 85704
(602)742-6455

GARDENS SOUTHWEST
P.O. Box 34308
Phoenix, AZ 85067
(602)234-0840
A publication of Phoenix Home & Garden Magazine.

PHOENIX HOME & GARDEN MAGAZINE
P.O. Box 34308
Phoenix, AZ 85067
(602)234-0840

SAN DIEGO HOME GARDEN
655 Fourth Avenue
San Diego, CA 92101
(619)233-4567

SUNSET MAGAZINE
80 Willow Road
Menlo Park, CA 94025
(415)321-3600

BIBLIOGRAPHY

Books

Arizona Chapter, Soil Conservation Society of America. *Landscaping With Native Arizona Plants.* Tucson, AZ: The University of Arizona Press, 1973.

Bock, Warren and Haase, Ynez. *Historical Atlas of New Mexico.* Norman, OK: University of Oklahoma Press, 1969.

Bogert, Frank M. *Palm Springs: First Hundred Years.* Palm Springs, CA: Palm Springs Heritage Associates, 1987.

Chilton, Katherine. *New Mexico: A New Guide to the Colorful State.* Albuquerque, NM: University of New Mexico Press, 1984.

Church, Thomas. *Gardens Are for People.* New York, NY: McGraw-Hill Book Company, 1983.

Cornett, Jim. *Coachella Valley Nature Guide.* Palm Springs, GA: Nature Trails Press, 1980.

Crawford, Stanley. *Mayordomo: Chronicle of an Acequia in Northern New Mexico.* Albuquerque, NM: University of New Mexico Press, 1988.

Dobyns, Winifred Starr. *California Gardens.* New York, NY: The MacMillan Company, 1931.

Eckbo, Garrett. *Landscape for Living.* New York, NY: F.W. Dodge Corporation, 1950.

Elmore, Francis H. *Shrubs and Trees of the Southwest Uplands.* Tucson, AZ: Southwest Parks And Monuments Association, 1976.

Hay, Roy, and Synge, Patrick M. *The Color Dictionary of Flowers and Plants.* New York, NY: Crown Publishers, Inc., 1969.

Jaeger, Edmund C. *The California Deserts.* Stanford, CA: Stanford University Press, 1965.

Lowe, Charles H. *Arizona's Natural Environment.* Tucson, AZ: The University of Arizona Press, 1964.

McAlester, Virginia, and Lee. *A Field Guide to American Houses.* New York, NY: Alfred A. Knopf, 1984.

McGuire, Diane Kostial. *Gardens of America: Three Centuries of Design.* Charlottesville, VA: Thomasson-Grant, 1989.

McKeever, Michael. *A Shrot History of San Diego.* San Francisco, CA: Lexikos, 1985.

MacPhail, Elizabeth C. *Kate Sessions, Pioneer Horticulturist.* San Diego, CA: San Diego Historical Society, 1976.

Morrow, Baker H. *A Dictionary of Landscape Architecture.* Albuquerque, NM: University of New Mexico Press, 1986.

Olin, George. *House in the Sun.* Tucson, AZ: Southwest Parks and Monuments Association, 1977.

Ortho Book Series. *The World of Cactus & Succulents.* San Francisco, CA: Ortho Books, 1977.

Padilla, Victoria. *Southern Californaia Gardens.* Berkeley and Los Angeles, CA: University of California Press, 1961.

Pereire, Anita. *The Prentice Hall Encyclopedia of Garden Flowers.* New York, NY: Prentice Hall Press, 1988.

Phillips, Judith. *Southwestern Landscaping With Native Plants.* Santa Fe, NM: Museum of New Mexico Press, 1987.

Pryde, Philip R. *San Diego: An Introduction to the Region.* Dubuque, IA: Kendall/Hunt Publishing Company, 1984.

Salt River Project. *The Taming of the Salt.* Phoenix, AZ: Salt River Project Publications, 1979.

Snyder, Ernest, *Arizona Outdoor Guide.* Phoenix, AZ: Golden West Publishers, 1985.

Spellenberg, Richard. *The Audubon Society Field Guide to North American Wildflowers, Western Region.* New York, NY: Alfred A. Knopf, 1979.

Ungnade, Herbert E. *Guide to the New Mexico Mountains.* Albuquerque, NM: University of New Mexico Press, 1965.

Valley Garden Center. *Practical Gardening in Southern Arizona.* Phoenix, AZ: Valley Garden Center, 1973.

Watts, Tom, and Watts, May Theilgaard, *Desert Tree Finder.* Berkeley, CA: Nature Study Guild, 1974.

Williams, Jerry L. *New Mexico in Maps.* Albuquerque, NM: University of New Mexico Press, 1988.

Williamson, Joseph F. *Sunset Western Garden Book.* Menlo Park, CA: Lane Publishing Company, 1988.

Yoch, James J. *Landscaping The American Dream.* New York, NY: Harry N. Abrams, Inc./Sagapress, Inc., 1989.

"Artistic Earthenscape." *Landscape Architecture* (Washington, DC), June 1989, pp. 64–68.

Cheek, Lawrence. "From Tucson With Love." *Arizona Highways Magazine* (Phoenix, AZ), February 1986, pp. 24–26.

Fish, Richard. "Walling Off the World." *Garden Design* (Washington, DC), Autumn 1988, pp. 34–41, 94.

Haven, Sharon. "Spiced-Up Spanish Modern." *Better Homes and Gardens Building Ideas* (Des Moines, IA), Winter 1988/89, pp. 33–42.

Morrow, Baker H. "Old Landscapes, New Ideas." *New Mexico Architecture* (Albuquerque, NM), September/October 1985, pp. 11–17.

Morrow, Baker H. "Stone and Spring in Torrance County: Three Classic New Mexico Landscapes." *Mass* (School of Architecture and Planning, University of New Mexico, Albuquerque, NM), Fall 1987, pp. 27–29.

"Palms in the High Desert." *Sunset Magazine* (Menlo Park, CA), May 1982, pp. 266–267.

"Palms That Mind Their Manners in Small Gardens." *Sunset Magazine* (Menlo Park, CA), March 1984, p. 210.

Rogers, Walter E. "Looking Backward to Cope With Water Shortages: A History of Native Plants in Southern Arizona." *Landscape Architecture* (Louisville, KY), May 1979, pp. 304–314.

Streatfield, David. "The Evolution of the California Landscape." *Landscape Architecture* (Louisville, KY). May 1977, pp. 229–249.

"These Are Palms That Behave Themselves." *Sunset Magazine* (Menlo Park, CA), June 1981, pp. 236–238.